Working in Statutory Contexts

SKILLS FOR CONTEMPORARY SOCIAL WORK

Tony Evans and Mark Hardy, *Evidence and Knowledge for Practice*
Andrew Hill, *Working in Statutory Contexts*

Working in Statutory Contexts

ANDREW HILL

polity

First published in 2010 by Polity Press

Polity Press
65 Bridge Street
Cambridge CB2 1UR, UK

Polity Press
350 Main Street
Malden, MA 02148, USA

ISBN-13: 978-0-7456-4269-7
ISBN-13: 978-0-7456-4270-3(pb)

A catalogue record for this book is available from the British Library.

Typeset in 10.5 on 12 pt Sabon
by Toppan Best-set Premedia Limited
Printed and bound in Great Britain by MPG Books Group Limited, Bodmin, Cornwall

The publisher has used its best endeavours to ensure that the URLs for external websites referred to in this book are correct and active at the time of going to press. However, the publisher has no responsibility for the websites and can make no guarantee that a site will remain live or that the content is or will remain appropriate.

Every effort has been made to trace all copyright holders, but if any have been inadvertently overlooked the publisher will be pleased to include any necessary credits in any subsequent reprint or edition.

For further information on Polity, visit our website: www.politybooks.com

Contents

Analytic Contents

List of Summaries of Skills

Acknowledgements

Many thanks are due to colleagues at the University of York and to others who read and commented on parts of the manuscript; Mark Hardy, Colin Hill, Andy Hosking, Juliet Koprowska, Ian Shaw and Sara Ward. Thanks also to Ian Shaw for his help in shaping the initial thinking, and to several anonymous reviewers for detailed comments.

Introduction

While I was writing this book, Tracey Connelly, the mother of a 17-month old child known as baby Peter, her boyfriend, Steven Barker, and Barker's brother, Jason Owen, were found guilty of causing baby Peter's death. It emerged that baby Peter's name had been on what was then the child protection register for the final eight months of his life, and that social workers had made regular visits to the family. Indeed there was a nine-month history of suspected non-accidental injuries, hospital admissions and police investigations (Guardian, 2008). This led to a period of intense public scrutiny of professional practice in this specific case and of child protection work more widely.

As I followed the media coverage and listened to the debate, I began to wonder about the impact of this case on potential readers of the present book. Although the book covers skills that are applicable in a wide range of statutory contexts, including mental health, community care and youth justice, nonetheless statutory child care and child protection represent a significant strand within it. This reflects not only my own background in child-care work, but also the fact that duties towards children under the Children Act 1989 are a high-profile element of the statutory context for social work. Baby Peter was the latest in a series of highly publicised cases where, on the face of it, there appeared to be a lack of skilled intervention.

Trying to be optimistic, I wondered whether the media coverage of the case of baby Peter might encourage more people to take an interest in developing the skills for what is often referred to as 'statutory work'. Here was a clear demonstration of the importance of such work, primarily of course to the vulnerable adults or children whom local authorities are charged with protecting, but also to society as a whole.

Yet, realistically, the media coverage of the case of baby Peter was hardly an advert for statutory social work. Who would want to get involved in difficult cases like that, with the risk of being blamed publicly if things go wrong? Not surprisingly, concerns about the adverse impact of the baby Peter case on social work recruitment were widely reported at the time (Andrew, 2008). But it remains my conviction that, despite – and perhaps because of – the obvious difficulties, statutory contexts for social work are very important. The need for highly skilled social workers to undertake statutory tasks in a wide variety of contexts has never been clearer.

So, in the light of baby Peter, I want to consider some fundamental questions about why people come into social work in the first place and what they think about the prospect of working in statutory contexts. This discussion of motivations and reservations will serve as an introduction to the central themes of the book: how social work in statutory contexts can be done ethically, and how it can be done well.

Reasons for Becoming a Social Worker

Why does anyone decide to become a social worker? Researchers have found that the most common reason given by applicants for social work training in the UK is the desire to help others and to improve people's quality of life (Furness, 2007). This fits with my own experience as a university admissions tutor for qualifying social work programmes: 'I want to make a difference' is a phrase I hear a lot. I am encouraged by this, since service to humanity is one of the five basic values of social work (BASW, 2002), and it was certainly one of my own reasons for becoming a social worker.

The second reason given was the expectation that social work will be a rewarding and a challenging career. But when does a challenge provide welcome interest and excitement, and when does it threaten to become unacceptably stressful, or even overwhelming? And where does statutory social work fit on such a scale?

My experience suggests that many of those applying to undertake social work training would prefer to work with people who clearly choose to be helped. They want to develop an open and trusting relationship, a shared understanding of the problems and a genuine partnership in tackling them. Of course, most applicants are aware that in statutory contexts things may be more difficult than this picture suggests. In the UK, local authorities have legal duties which mean that social workers must work with vulnerable people and their families and carers even when social work help has not been sought. Or they may have to apply strict access criteria when people ask for statutory care services. In these circumstances people may be hostile to social workers; individuals may be suffering from mental illness, they may misuse drugs, they may conceal histories of concern and, of course, they may conceal the abuse of children. Many trainee social workers have worries and reservations about working in statutory contexts.

Let me make it clear that I am not complaining about these reservations. This was my own position when I started out in social work, and it still seems to me to be a perfectly reasonable one. Wanting to help people and to make a difference is relatively straightforward when people ask for help and services are plentiful. Skills for such work, for example counselling skills, are well understood. But in statutory contexts trainee social workers may be wise to have concerns about the difficulties of acquiring the skills for working effectively with potentially challenging people and about the aims and ethics of doing social work with those who have not sought help, or in situations where services are tightly rationed.

Concerns about Being Able to Do the Job Well

Doing social work in statutory contexts often involves making difficult professional judgements when strong emotions are being felt by everyone involved. Should an adult be admitted compulsorily to hospital for assessment? Should an application be made for an emergency protection order? Are an older person's needs enough to warrant the admission to a residential care home that the family is seeking? Fear is perhaps the most significant of the emotions involved. Chris Beckett (2007) names some of the different types of fear that social workers may experience. There is:

- fear of causing upset
- fear of making a mistake and being blamed
- fear of the anger and hostility of others
- sometimes even fear for one's own physical safety.

Following the coverage of the case of baby Peter and a highly personalised campaign in some parts of the media against some of those involved, fears about getting the blame if things go wrong seem particularly realistic. After all, as Ferguson (2008) has argued bravely, detecting human cruelty is deeply disturbing, emotional work where there will always be some human error. Given that all these fears are realistic, the question is whether the organisational context for such work can contain them. Or to put it another way: will I get the support I need in order to cope with the emotional content of the work, to make good judgements and to keep myself and others safe?

I am afraid that there is no easy reassurance to be given here. The case of baby Peter has also raised concerns about the organisation of statutory social work in the London Borough of Haringey and, by implication, elsewhere. Does understaffing mean excessive workloads for social workers? Are social workers well trained, managed and supported? Do social workers spend too much time on the completion of new online assessment forms and not enough time in face-to-face contact with the people they are working with? As I write this, the government has set up a Social Work Taskforce in response to the case of baby Peter and other serious case reviews elsewhere in the UK. According to the press release, the taskforce will undertake a comprehensive review of frontline social work practice and identify any barriers that social workers face in doing their jobs effectively, including the implementation of new IT systems (Department for Children, Schools and Families, 2009).

One of the key themes of the present book is the relationship between the practice skills of individual social workers and the organisational context in which they work. We need to pay attention to both if we are to practise well.

A second theme is the relationship between social work skills that are needed in statutory contexts and those needed in other social work contexts. Part of the rationale for this book is the argument that statutory contexts sometimes demand additional skills or, perhaps more frequently, a different application of skills which are common in all social work, and that this is not sufficiently recognised. As we consider skills for statutory contexts we will pay attention to similarities and differences with social work practice in other contexts.

Concerns about Aims and Ethics

So far we have considered concerns about *how* social work in statutory contexts can be done. But there is a second set of concerns, which relate more to the aims and ethics of the work. These are questions about *why* social work in statutory contexts should be done at all.

There has long been a radical critique of social work, and particularly of its statutory functions. Part of the critique is that the element of social control which is inherent in many statutory functions is focused unjustly on poor and oppressed groups. Black people are over-represented in compulsory admissions to mental health units. Poor people are more likely to have their children made subject to child protection plans. According to this view, the individualisation inherent in the casework approach blames – and even punishes – individuals for social problems whose origins lie primarily in unjust social structures. It also undermines the kind of corporate action that might lead to social change.

In response to this situation, some proponents of anti-oppressive social work argue that it is possible to practise individual casework in such a way as to counter, or at least take account of, the effects of structural oppression even in statutory contexts. However, there are obvious tensions between some of the principles of anti-oppressive practice, for example the principle of empowering service users, and the legitimate aims of statutory social work that might include controlling abusive behaviour.

A third theme of the book is how skills for social work in statutory contexts fit with the values of social work as a profession and with the specific aims of statutory work. What do we mean by anti-oppressive practice in statutory contexts?

How the Book Is Organised

Part I considers issues of context. The main legal jurisdiction covered here is that of England and Wales, although the skills under discussion are transferable to other jurisdictions. The reader is referred to equivalent legislation in Scotland and Northern Ireland where this is appropriate. Chapter 1 opens with an account of the legal basis of social work and its relationship to the notion of 'statutory work'. It then considers current issues in the organisational context for such work, picking up concerns about doing difficult emotional work in stressful organisational settings. This discussion forms the background to a later chapter on skills for working in organisations. Chapter 2 turns to the concerns about the aims and ethics of social work in statutory contexts. It makes suggestions about how anti-oppressive practice may be conceptualised and carried out in contexts in which controlling another person's behaviour may be what is required by law.

Ideas about the application of anti-oppressive practice in statutory settings run right through Part II, which considers a series of skills.

These are organised according to a notional, temporal sequence of casework, from meeting and engaging with those with whom social workers will work, to assessing and planning, court work, promoting change, ending, evaluating and reflective practice. Each skill is cross-referenced to the relevant National Occupational Standards for Social Work, and these are listed in full in the appendix (pp. 180–182). However, it should be clear that social work does not always proceed in this strict sequence. Reflection, for example, is discussed at the end of the book, but in practice it is certainly not to be restricted to after the event. And the processes of assessment and of promoting change often happen simultaneously, continuously reinforcing each other. However, a certain amount of disentangling of interlocking processes helps in analysis; besides, books can only be presented in a linear sequence, even if they are rarely written or read in that way.

Each chapter includes at least one case example. All the case examples are invented. They serve to embed thinking about skills in a specific practice context. Each chapter starts with a brief summary of its contents and ends with some suggestions for further reading. Each chapter also contains exercises, which can be done individually or in groups.

Statutory Contexts as an Integral Part of Social Work

In this introduction I have identified some common concerns about how social work in statutory contexts can be done ethically, and how it can be done well. These concerns will be considered throughout the book, as we examine both context and skills. But the fact is that, sooner or later, in whatever country they practise, social workers are likely to face the realities of working in statutory contexts, because such contexts represent an integral part of the professional role. In England, the Department of Health requires that all social workers in training gain experience of 'statutory social work tasks involving legal interventions' (Department of Health, 2002c: 11). Similar requirements apply in Scotland and Northern Ireland. These statutory functions may not be all there is to social work, but they are an essential component of it. Social workers need to develop skills for working in statutory contexts. Whilst it is clear that practice skills cannot be acquired just by reading books, nonetheless I hope that the present one will support and encourage the development of skills in such an important, challenging and potentially rewarding area of social work.

Part I
Context

1

Legal and Organisational Context

Chapter summary

This chapter outlines the statutory basis of social work and explains what is meant by 'social work in statutory contexts'. It goes on to consider the organisational contexts for such work and some of the pressures on the agencies undertaking it.

The Legal Context

The statutory basis of social work in England and Wales is contained in the Local Authority Social Services Act 1970 (LASSA). Schedule 1 to that Act lists each Act of Parliament that imposes a statutory function on local authorities, together with a brief account of those functions. Local authorities do not have any choice in this; the duties in question are a part of their core functions as laid down by Parliament. The full list of statutory functions is updated regularly, as new legislation is enacted and becomes available online (Ministry of Justice, 2002). Table 1.1 is an edited version of the full list, showing the major legislation. (The Social Work (Scotland) Act 1968 gives a similar list of statutory functions to Scottish local authorities.)

The phrase 'statutory work' is used by social workers to describe social work that *must* be carried out in order for their legal duties to be fulfilled. Typically, people on the receiving end of statutory social work have not asked for help and they may have limited choice in the matter, or even none at all. They are sometimes referred to as 'involuntary clients'.

Table 1.1 Edited version of Local Authority Social Services Act 1970, Schedule 1

Enactments Conferring Functions Assigned to Social Services Committees	
Enactment	Nature of functions
National Assistance Act 1948	
Sections 21 to 27	Provision of residential accommodation for the aged, infirm, needy, etc.
Sections 29 and 30	Welfare of persons who are blind, deaf, dumb or otherwise handicapped or are suffering from mental disorder; use of voluntary organisations for administration of welfare schemes.
Sections 43 to 45	Recovery of costs of providing certain services.
Disabled Persons (Employment) Act 1958	
Section 3	Provision of facilities for enabling disabled persons to be employed or work under special conditions.
Health Services and Public Health Act 1968	
Section 45	Promotion of welfare of old people.
Children and Young Persons Act 1969	
The whole Act except section 9 in so far as they assign functions to a local authority in their capacity of a local education authority.	Care and other treatment of children and young persons through court proceedings.
Chronically Sick and Disabled Persons Act 1970	
Section 1	Obtaining information as to need for, and publishing information as to existence of, certain welfare services.
Section 2	Provision of certain welfare services.
Mental Health Act 1983	
Parts II, III and VI	Welfare of the mentally disordered; guardianship of persons suffering from mental disorder including such persons removed to England and Wales from Scotland or Northern Ireland; exercise of functions of nearest relative of person so suffering.
Sections 66, 67, 69(1)	Exercise of functions of nearest relative in relation to applications and references to Mental Health Review Tribunals.
Section 114	Appointment of approved social workers.

Table 1.1 *Continued*

Enactments Conferring Functions Assigned to Social Services Committees	
Enactment	**Nature of functions**
Section 115	Entry and inspection.
Section 116	Welfare of certain hospital patients.
Section 117	After-care of detained patients.
Health and Social Services and Social Security Adjudications Act 1983	
Section 17	Charges for local authority welfare services
Housing Act 1996	
Section 213(1)(b)	Co-operation in relation to homeless persons and persons threatened with homelessness.
Disabled Persons (Services, Consultation and Representation) Act 1986	
Sections 1 to 5, 7 and 8	Representation and assessment of disabled persons.
Children Act 1989	
The whole Act, in so far as it confers functions on a local authority within the meaning of that Act.	Welfare reports. Consent to application for residence order in respect of child in care. Family assistance orders. Functions under Part III of the Act (local authority support for children and families). Care and supervision. Protection of children. Functions in relation to community homes, voluntary homes and voluntary organisations, private children's homes, private arrangements for fostering children, child minding and day care for young children.
National Health Service and Community Care Act 1990	
Section 46	Preparation of plans for community care services.
Section 47	Assessment of needs for community care services.
Carers (Recognition and Services) Act 1995	
Section 1	Assessment of ability of carers to provide care.
Carers and Disabled Children Act 2000	
The whole Act, in so far as it confers functions on a local authority within the meaning of that Act.	Assessment of carers' needs. Provision of services to carers. Provision of vouchers.

Table 1.1 *Continued*

Enactments Conferring Functions Assigned to Social Services Committees	
Enactment	Nature of functions
Health and Social Care Act 2001 Part 4, in so far as it confers functions on a local authority in England or Wales within the meaning of that Part.	Functions in relation to the provision of residential accommodation. Making of direct payments to person in respect of his securing provision of community care services or services to carers.
Adoption and Children Act 2002	Maintenance of Adoption Service; functions of local authority as adoption agency.

SOURCE Edited version of online table from UK Statute Law Database: http://www. statutelaw.gov.uk/content.aspx?LegType=All+Primary&PageNumber=11&NavFro m=2&activeTextDocId=538583&parentActiveTextDocId=538583&linkToATDocu mentId=477582&linkToATVersionNumber=17&showProsp=1&#813914

Table 1.1 contains functions that are, clearly, examples of statutory work. These include:

- protection of children under the Children Act 1989
- work with 'looked after' children under the Children Act 1989
- work in Youth Offending Teams under the Children and Young Persons Act 1969
- reporting to court under the Children Act 1989
- some duties under the Mental Health Act 1983.

In all these cases the local authority has specific duties to carry out. Those affected by them are not likely to have sought help but, rather, to have had social work imposed on them. For these people the consequences of not cooperating, at least to some extent, with social workers may be so serious that they have little choice in the matter. Young people who have offended may be taken back to court; parents may find that their children remain in local authority care.

However, even in these circumstances we should not assume that the exercise of legal powers leads to straightforward compliance. It is common for people to find ways of resisting social work interventions, to a greater or lesser extent. In other circumstances many liberal-minded social workers might celebrate such resistance to authority. It might even be seen as evidence of empowerment. But in statutory contexts social workers must be clear about the aims and ethics of their work in order to decide how to respond.

Note that social workers do not have much choice in the matter either. They can't just withdraw from statutory work because the young person is angry and doesn't want to see them, or because the parent resists all their attempts to help. In a different way, they too are constrained by the legal imperative.

But not all of the functions prescribed by the LASSA 1970 and listed in Table 1.1 are examples of social work that is imposed on people. Table 1.1 also gives the local authorities a duty to provide statutory social work services of a kind that is *not* usually imposed. Examples include:

- welfare services under Section 2 of the Chronically Sick and Disabled Persons Act 1970
- support for children and families under Part III of the Children Act 1989
- provision of services to carers under the Carers and Disabled Children Act 2000.

The local authority has a statutory duty to offer these services, and people are free to use them or not, as they choose. But, amongst social workers, use of the phrase 'statutory work' tends to be reserved for social work that is, to some extent at least, imposed on people. It is often equated with 'involuntary' work. Free-to-choose support services are frequently not understood as being statutory work, despite the fact that such services have a clear statutory basis. This misuse of language is unhelpful in several ways. First, it underplays the significance of the role that social workers have in advocating on behalf of service users who must demonstrate their entitlement to statutory community care services. Despite the publication of eligibility criteria for access to adult community care services (Department of Health, 2002b), this remains a contentious area of statutory social work. Second, this misuse reflects and legitimises the relative lack of priority given to vital support services that people are free to choose, even in the statutory context. In relation to child protection work, the need to refocus on statutory support services was one of the *Messages from Research* (Department of Health, 1995a). A similar conclusion was reached more recently by Lord Laming in his review of child protection services after the death of baby Peter (Laming, 2009). Finally, it is simply confusing to equate statutory work just with imposed or involuntary social work.

All local authority social work is statutory work

The truth is that all local authority social work is, in an important sense, statutory work. As we have seen, local authorities and other public bodies in the UK have their powers (things they *can* do) and their duties (things they *must* do) set for them by central government. They are not allowed to do anything else; that would be to exceed their powers, and it would be illegal. Local authorities must be able to point to legislation that enables them to provide even those services that people are free to choose. It is important not to lose sight of the statutory basis of local authority free-to-choose services. If the term 'statutory work' is used in ways that exclude them, then it is misleading.

Exercise 1.1

Throughout their working day, local authority social workers should be able to point to the legislation that gives them either the power or the duty to carry out their current task. Here are today's diary commitments for social workers Sue and Mike, working in England. Work out what legislation gives the relevant power or duty for each activity. You can refer to Table 1.1 for relevant Acts, but you may need to refer to the legislation itself in order to find the relevant subsections. (The full text of the legislation is available on the Office of Public Sector Information at www.opsi.gov.uk). Answers are at the end of the chapter.

Appointment Time	Sue	Mike
09.00	Call in at the local family centre to attend a review of a support package to a single parent	Visit a couple at their home after their request for help in caring for their adult son, who has a learning disability
11.00	Attend a child protection case conference	Write a care plan
15.00	Make a home visit to arrange support for a young mother following her discharge from a mental hospital	Discuss the provision of direct payments to a young woman who is deaf

---

It is also important to note that statutory social work is not confined to local authorities. Patterns of service delivery are changing all the time. It is becoming increasingly common for local authorities to form partnerships with a range of voluntary or third-sector organisations, designed to deliver some of the statutory functions of the former. Examples include private fostering agencies, or work done in voluntary child care organisations to support care leavers. In addition, the law gives statutory functions to organisations other than local authorities. For example, social workers employed by the National Society for the Prevention of Cruelty to Children (NSPCC) may be authorised by the Secretary of State under the Children Act 1989 to undertake enquiries under section 47 (s.47) and to apply to the court for orders.

Voluntary and involuntary

As we have seen, one of the negative consequences of restricting the phrase 'statutory work' to make it refer only to social work which is imposed on people is that this overlooks social work's role in helping people to gain voluntary access to statutory support services, particularly to adult community care services. But, even in relation to involuntary social work, there is a further difficulty with the use of the phrase – a difficulty that is significant throughout this whole book.

The equation of 'statutory' work and 'non-statutory' work with 'involuntary' and 'voluntary' appears to imply the existence of two distinct categories. One of the themes of this book is to question ways of thinking that create binary categories: in this case, statutory work that is involuntary from the perspective of service users and non-statutory work that is voluntary. In most social work settings, things are more complex than this. Consider case example 1.1.

Case example 1.1

A Health Visitor's concerns about John, aged 2, led to an enquiry under s.47 of the Children Act 1989. (This is the section that describes the circumstances in which a local authority in England and Wales has a duty to make enquires to establish whether there is a need to take action to safeguard a child's welfare. In Scotland there is a similar provision under the Children (Scotland) Act 1995). The reported concerns were that Julie, a young, white, single parent, had little support from family or friends and a low level of parenting skills. Specifically, John had a persistent nappy rash and his speech appeared to be delayed. He also had some bruising on his upper arm.

The enquiry included a medical examination. It established an accidental cause for the bruising. The remaining concerns were not felt to be so serious as to warrant the holding of an Initial Child Protection Case Conference. Nonetheless the enquiry recommended that Julie should be encouraged to attend a weekly parenting programme and that a local volunteer should try to help Julie to make use of local support such as a parents' drop-in group.

Julie was initially angry and upset. She was reluctant to attend the parenting programme, but she was worried about what might happen if she didn't. In fact Julie found the programme helpful and enjoyable, and she made some friends. She signed up for a second course after the social worker had stopped visiting.

The s.47 enquiry fits the definition of statutory work, and Julie may be thought of as an 'involuntary client' whilst that enquiry was taking place. But the fact that it did not lead to an Initial Child Protection Case Conference is a clear indication that the enquiry did not provide evidence of significant harm. In these circumstances the local authority had no grounds for further legal action, even if Julie had refused to accept the proposed help. What happened after the enquiry was purely voluntary. So it seems that statutory work can include elements, or contain stages, that are not compulsory. But note that, from Julie's point of view, the distinction was not obvious. Julie experienced this offer of help as, to some extent, coercive. After all, it followed a formal investigation, and Julie was not sure that she could really afford to refuse to attend the programme.

This illustrates some of the complexities. Support services are often highly relevant in statutory contexts, and sometimes the strict legal position may be that people are entirely free to choose whether or not to use them. But they may be 'encouraged' to do so, and they may experience this persuasion as, to a greater or lesser extent, coercive and to be resisted.

By the way, the positive ending of this story is not intended to imply that such outcomes are typical, or even that the use of statutory power can have benign outcomes. The argument is that individual casework cannot be simply categorised as involuntary or voluntary. These categories are not fixed and do not equate to statutory and non-statutory work. Things change over time, and people's subjective experiences of the degree of coercion may bear little relation to the strict legal position. Social work in statutory contexts often includes offers of support that people are free to accept or reject, perhaps running alongside interventions that are clearly imposed. However, the overall statutory context may be experienced as coercive, and this may lead to resistance that affects the process of giving and taking help. It is vital to understand the interplay of statutory power, persuasion, resistance and cooperation at the local level, in relation to the stages of individual casework. It forms the background to many of the skills considered in Part II.

Because of these difficulties in the use of the phrase 'statutory work', the present book mostly uses the alternative phrase 'social work in statutory contexts'. This formula is intended to cover any social work setting where the primary driver for the work is the need to determine whether or not the local authority has a legal duty towards an individual and, if so, to carry it out. Some social work in statutory contexts may be in response to a request for a statutory support service, for example in relation to community care services. Very often such a request will come directly from the person involved and, from that person's perspective, the acceptance of any service offered will be entirely voluntary. On other occasions, the local authority may be alerted to individuals whom they may have a legal duty to protect, or to protect the public from. Examples include child protection work, youth justice work and duties under mental health legislation. Such alerts are more likely to come from third parties than from the individuals themselves. In these contexts some interventions are likely to be imposed; but, even here, the local authority may also offer statutory support services that are not imposed. Yet, despite the clarity of the underlying legal position, the individuals affected may experience considerable ambiguity about which is which.

Use of language to refer to those affected

Finding a satisfactory term for people who are subject to, or affected by, the statutory functions of social work is difficult. The difficulties are part of a wider debate about how to describe anyone with whom social workers practise. The term 'client' has its roots in traditional social work values and therapeutic approaches, whereas the phrase preferred in the current mainstream social work literature in the UK is 'service user'. This phrase reflects a view of people as citizens and consumers rather than as recipients of welfare. However, in statutory contexts both descriptions are problematic, since they seem to imply a voluntary relationship with the social worker that does not tell the full story.

The phrase 'involuntary clients' is used in the US (Ivanoff et al., 1994; Rooney, 1992) and sometimes in the UK (Trotter, 2006). But, once again, it implies a clear binary distinction between voluntary and involuntary, when, as we have seen, things may be more complex than that. This book makes use of phrases such as 'the people involved' or 'those concerned' when referring specifically to social work in statutory contexts. However, at times there is also discussion of social work as a whole, particularly in Chapter 2. There the language used reflects the social work practice being discussed; 'client' when discussing traditional and therapeutic approaches to social work, and 'service user' when discussing current approaches to anti-oppressive practice in the UK.

The Organisational Context

In statutory contexts the relevant legal powers and duties are given to public bodies and not to individual social workers. For example, in England and Wales it is the *local authority's* duty under the Children Act 1989 to safeguard and promote the welfare of children in need. Social workers carrying out these legal duties are doing so on behalf of their employing organisations. Whilst acting in a professional capacity they are subject nonetheless to the managerial control of the organisation. Decisions about how to carry out the local authority's statutory duties are not the sole responsibility of individual workers and are taken in consultation with managers. Social workers are often referred to as 'bureau-professionals' and contrasted with doctors, lawyers or ministers of religion, whose professional judgements are not managed in quite the same way.

Managerial limits on social workers' freedom of professional action can create tensions. There may be occasions when an agency policy or a management instruction appears to the social workers to be against the interests of the person they are working with. In such circumstances social workers have a professional responsibility towards service users that may involve taking a critical stance towards the agency. However, social workers also have responsibilities as employees towards their employer. Working creatively in the interests of service users in the midst of such tensions requires considerable skills. We will examine these skills when considering the use of supervision and agency procedures in Chapter 4. But first we need to consider some of the key organisational features of social work in statutory contexts.

Social work continues to change so rapidly that attempts to describe current patterns of service delivery are in danger of becoming outdated almost as soon as they are written. In the UK, new partnerships are being formed between health, education and social care with the establishment of Children's Trusts. Multidisciplinary teams deliver a changing pattern of health and social care services to adults in the context of evolving partnerships with users and carers, and with the third sector. Rather than try to offer a snapshot of how social work in statutory contexts is currently organised, it may be more helpful to trace some of the trends and to consider their implications.

Privatisation and marketisation

These terms refer to the processes of change since the 1980s, in which a variety of different providers of services have begun to compete with one another. This situation contrasts with the previous one, in which social services were mostly planned and provided by the state. In the process:

- clients become customers and gain a greater choice of services
- statutory bodies become purchasers instead of providers of services, creating competition
- they become regulators, not planners
- administrators become managers, being responsible for controlling costs
- allocation gives way to competition as a way of spending public money on services (Drakeford, 2000).

Marketisation has also led to an increased emphasis on enterprise and entrepreneurship in social work and to the incorporation of business practice and language (Harris, 2003; Pinker, 1990).

Managerialism

At the same time, managerialism has also had a significant impact on the public sector (Clarke et al., 2000; Kirkpatrick et al., 2005). It has been argued that management in local authority social services departments in the 1970s and early 1980s was relatively weak, considerable power being exercised by the social workers themselves (Harris, 1998). Managerialism under the Thatcher government, continuing under New Labour, is often presented as a challenge to professional power, with management's right to manage being forcefully asserted. Target setting and other rationalist management techniques have been applied in a way that many regard as deskilling for social work professionals. Codified procedures that make increasing use of information technology and check-box forms are widely held to have led to a reductionist version of social work, which fails to understand the complex and often ambiguous relationships between social workers and service users (Dominelli, 2004). In the process, social workers have become subject to much greater management control and surveillance.

But it may be an oversimplification to suggest that the interests of managers and social workers are always in opposition. In social work, progression to managerial roles has always been a major career path for professionals, and most managers continue to be qualified and experienced social workers. Exworthy and Halford (1999) argue that the new managerialism opens the way for new relationships between social workers and their managers through its emphasis on entrepreneurship, decentralisation, and the enabling of staff to make their own contribution. We will examine skills for working creatively in such an environment in Chapter 3.

Modernisation

One of the key features of the Labour government's agenda for change has been the stress on the modernisation of social services (Department of Health, 1998). Modernisation has included the strong encouragement of partnerships between agencies to 'create new shared ways of delivering services that are individually tailored, accessible and more joined up' (Department of Health, 2000a: 30). Health and social care have been brought closer together, for example in England in Care Trusts, under s.45 of the Health and Social Care Act 2001. Similarly, children's trusts are a response to the duty to cooperate under the Children Act 2004. They bring together all the services for children and young people, so that '[p]eople will work in effective multidisciplinary teams, be trained jointly to tackle cultural and professional divides, use a lead professional model where many disciplines are involved, and be co-located, often in extended schools or children's centres' (Department for Children, Schools and Families 2005).

But joined-up thinking extends beyond public bodies. Partnerships are also being encouraged between the statutory, private and voluntary sectors and with service users and their carers, although these are not without their difficulties (Langan, 2000).

Modernisation has also included the increasing use of information and communication technology (ICT), both for communication and for managing data – about staff and service users alike. However, there is no easy resolution to the apparently contradictory demands of openness and information-sharing between agencies on the one hand, and the demands of confidentiality and protection of personal information on the other. There are potential benefits as well as real dangers here, in the growth of surveillance; and, in the end, it is perhaps the impact of ICT on practice that is important (Gould, 2003).

Regulation and inspection

'In all areas, monitoring and inspection are playing a key role, as an incentive to higher standards. [. . .] A new pragmatism is growing in the relations between public and private sector. The emphasis must be on goals not rules, and monitoring achievements not processes' (Blair, 1998: 16–17).

This observation by Tony Blair encapsulates the relationship between inspection, the modernising theme of joined-up services working together in partnership, and a pragmatic emphasis on outcomes. Certainly in the personal social services there has been a proliferation of different ways in which standards are measured and controlled. These include:

- performance indicators for local government
- the establishment in 2001 of the Social Care Institute for Excellence (SCIE)
- the establishment in 2004 of the Commission for Social Care Inspection (CSCI)
- the legal protection of the title 'social worker' from April 2005 under the Care Standards Act 2000.

Once again, the consequences may be mixed. Services may improve as provision becomes more standardised across the UK and as social workers are trained and registered to do the job. Yet these may also be seen as top-down developments, implying increased surveillance and control of social workers, of their education and of their practice (Cree, 2002).

Exercise 1.2

Think of an organisation known to you that delivers social work services and has been in existence for some time. It may be large or small, statutory or voluntary, or in the third sector. Find out about its history over roughly the past ten years and assess the impact you think the processes of marketisation, managerialism, modernisation, regulation and inspection have had on the way it delivers its services.

Pressures on Organisations with Statutory Functions

The processes of marketisation, managerialism, modernisation and regulation affect the whole of social work. This section considers two of the pressures on organisations that are most significant in statutory contexts, although they are not confined to them.

Accountability

There is no doubt that public and professional accountability is, quite properly, a vital component of ethical social work in statutory contexts. So, although processes designed to ensure accountability may be experienced as placing statutory organisations under pressure, this should not be read as a complaint. Of course, the media coverage of social work can be extremely hostile, and the profession often appears to be in the firing line. But this should not undermine the commitment of social workers to the principle of accountability. This section considers the following questions:

- If the pressures associated with accountability are more intense in statutory contexts than in others, then why is this so?
- What impact does this pressure have on the behaviour of organisations and on social work practice?
- How can any negative effects be minimised?

All professions have a commitment to serve their clients or service users and an associated duty to account to those people for the actions that they take (Banks, 2002). For social workers in the UK, this principle is enshrined in the professional code of ethics (BASW, 2002: 7). This applies equally to all the contexts of social work. But it is the notion of accountability to the wider public that, whilst present in all social work, puts the most intense pressure on statutory

functions – for example on protecting vulnerable people, on controlling dangerous people or on providing fair access to statutory
services.

First there is the question of maintaining public confidence. When
things go wrong, public inquiries will ask whether procedures were
followed, whether instructions from management were complied
with, whether ethical decisions were taken and whether practice was
technically competent. (Note that commentators such as Ferguson
(2004) have rightly questioned the level of public expectation, asking
whether the technology of child protection, in particular, is capable
of delivering an infallible blanket of protection.) It has been argued
that procedure-driven notions of accountability are one of the reasons
for the increasing management surveillance of practice, for example
by measuring outputs and by collecting a variety of monitoring data
(Banks, 2004).

Second, there is the question of how the rights of individuals can
be upheld when such individuals feel that they have been badly
treated by statutory social work. Understandably, some of those who
find themselves subject to the controlling or rationing functions of
social work feel that they should appeal or complain. Case example
1.2 explores some of the dilemmas.

Case example 1.2

Alice and Elsie are two white British sisters, aged 85 and 80, who live
together in rented accommodation in England. Alice, the elder one, has
significant memory loss and is at increasing risk of falls. Following an
assessment by a social worker from the Local Authority Older Persons'
Service, it was decided that Alice cannot be safely supported at home. It
was agreed with Alice and her family that a residential care home placement is required.

Elsie, the younger sister, is in much better health, though she does
experience a lot of anxiety. She does not want to be separated from Alice
and wishes to move to the care home with her. Other family members
also feel that this would be best for both sisters. However, the social
worker's assessment is that Elsie can continue to be supported at home,
alone, through care services.

The family decided to make a complaint and the first, internal, stage
of the complaints procedure was triggered. A local authority service
manager looked at all the details of the assessment and upheld the social
worker's decision. The family was still unhappy, however, and took the

complaint to stage two. This involved the Local Government Ombudsman. When the ombudsman examined Elsie's case, it was clear that the
local authority had correctly followed the requirements of the NHS and
Community Care Act 1990 and subsequent guidance (Department of
Health, 2002b). The Ombudsman found no reason to suppose that the
assessment outcome was inappropriate.

In this case example Elsie was upset about the decision that had been
taken and her family was angry. The family members believed that
the assessment was unfair because it did not appear to take into
account the relationship between the two sisters. They felt that it
failed to take into account their belief that Elsie would become more
anxious by living alone. So what were the options? Well, the decision
was taken internally by the local authority under the NHS and Community Care Act 1990. If, as in this case, a complaint is made, then
the decision must be reviewed internally, by a member of staff who
was not previously involved. A distinction is often drawn between
reviewing the process by which the decision was taken and reviewing
the decision itself. At this internal stage the person undertaking the
review must do both – that is, check both that the correct procedures
were followed and that the decision itself was the correct one, in the
light of all the facts.

If the complaint is not resolved at the internal stage, then the case
can be reviewed by the Local Government Ombudsman. (For other
United Kingdom nations, parallel duties are carried out by the Public
Services Ombudsman for Wales, by the Scottish Public Services
Ombudsman for Scotland and by the Northern Ireland Ombudsman
for Northern Ireland.) This second stage is limited to reviewing the
process by which the decision was taken. The ombudsman will not
question the merits of decisions taken or of professional judgements
made, provided that they were reached properly. Decisions can be
overturned by the ombudsman, but only if the assessment process
was flawed – for example, if key information was not sought, if carers
were not involved or if there was undue delay. Yet in Elsie's case it
is unlikely that the family will be satisfied with the ombudsman's
finding that the process was followed correctly. This is because their
complaint was really about the decision itself. There is a need for
clarity and openness about what can be considered at the internal
stage, and by the ombudsman.

So what is the impact on social workers of being held to account
in this way in statutory contexts? What is it like to live with the

likelihood that your work might be challenged and scrutinised in forensic detail by colleagues, by the ombudsman, and in some cases by the courts? One danger is that the fear of being criticised or blamed may lead to defensive practice. This is practice where the primary objective is to cover your back by playing it safe and by ensuring not only that the relevant procedures have been followed, but that there is a clear record of your having done so (Harris, 1987). Following the procedures is necessary, but there are dangers when workers' interests in not being blamed override their commitment to the primary task. Thompson (2005) points to the increased tensions between workers and service users, and Banks (2006) points out that there is a risk of doing your duty towards the agency, rather than what is morally right. A related danger is that a proliferation of procedures and standards may become unworkable. Banks' (2004) study suggests that some workers feel that there are too many procedures and these are too prescriptive and inflexible, and so they get in the way of sensitive and trusting relationships with service users. On the other hand, the same study shows that other workers see the positive benefits of this level of accountability. In their view, it gives clarity and focus to the work, with procedures providing a framework within which there remains significant professional autonomy. These workers welcomed the strengthening of the rights of service users.

This is not just a case of two different ways of looking at the same reality: glass being half-full or half-empty. Skilled social workers practise in ways that maximise the possibility that increased accountability will lead to positive outcomes. This starts with skills for using supervision and continues with skills for using agency procedures (both to be discussed in Chapter 3). And there is a strong case for arguing that, for example, the discipline of having to prepare a case for court promotes the development of a number of other highly desirable social work skills, as we shall see in Chapter 6, when looking at skills for court work.

Emotional content

In some situations social workers may exercise considerable power, for example in carrying out orders made by courts. But, perhaps strangely, in these situations social workers rarely feel powerful. This is very difficult work, and the subjective experience is more often one of fear. It might include fear of getting the blame, fear of hostile service users, or fear of causing or facing distress (Beckett, 2007). But it is not just fear that may be experienced. Jordan writes in strong terms about some of the other powerful feelings that arise in statutory work:

> [The social worker] [. . .] is usually beset by an overwhelming feeling of personal discomfort, of shame or terror or both. He is sickened by the implicit or explicit violence he is using, yet he is probably equally furious with the client who provoked it, often by violence of his own. He is horribly aware both of his power and his vulnerability. He feels simultaneously an agent of a brutal authority and a weak, exposed, inadequate person. (Jordan, 1979: 68)

Experiencing some of these intense and complex emotions is a normal and integral part of doing statutory social work. They come with the territory, so that even the most experienced or skilled workers cannot avoid having these feelings altogether. But, as well as understanding their normality and ubiquity, it is just as important that we understand that coping with the impact of such feelings is an issue for statutory social work agencies, and not just for the individual workers. Strong emotions can affect the behaviour of organisations as much as the behaviour of individuals. There are skills for individuals to learn in relation to managing these feelings, and we will turn to these in Chapter 3; but these skills can only be developed in the context of an agency that itself understands the significance of such intense emotions and is able to cope with them.

Much of what has been written about emotional stress on human service organisations and on the individuals working in them draws on psychodynamic theory (for example Obholzer and Roberts, 1994). On this view, organisations and individuals develop unconscious defences that act to protect them from the anxiety induced by strong feelings. Such defence mechanisms include:

- *Depersonalising* Menzies' (1988) classic study of nursing showed how the use of impersonal labels such as 'the hysterectomy in bed nine' helps to avoid the anxiety induced by personal contact with real people.

- *Using hierarchy for difficult decisions* The same study noted the tendency to avoid or to share responsibility for unpopular decisions. A common pattern is for junior staff to have most contact with patients or service users but to take least responsibility for decisions; whilst the reverse is true for senior staff. This has the effect of distancing senior decision-makers from the emotional impact of difficult decisions, whilst allowing junior staff to interact with patients or service users without being blamed by them for those decisions.

- *Using excessive caution* This is the tendency to play safe in decision-making, so as to limit anxiety.

- *Relying on procedures* We have already noted how the need for accountability promotes a reliance on procedures. The need to limit anxiety is another factor that leads in the same direction.

Whilst effective in limiting anxiety, some of these defences also have negative consequences. Such consequences become seriously problematic when the defences themselves grow rigid and impermeable, so that appropriate reactions to feelings are blocked, or when they extend so as to encompass imaginary anxieties (Hughes and Pengelly, 1997).

For example, it is common practice for organisational team structures to separate the early stages of statutory work, including the decision to intervene, from the longer-term follow-up work. Intake or assessment teams often transfer people to other social workers, for example, after an Initial Child Protection Case Conference. This structure insulates the workers who made the key decisions and protects them from the ongoing emotional impact; and, to some extent, it also absolves the new workers from the responsibility of, for example, having called the case conference. But this arrangement may become dysfunctional if it is too rigid. There is a danger that the individual concerned may feel that decisions about her have been taken by remote, impersonal forces and that talking to her new social worker is a waste of time. There is a danger that the new social worker may feel deskilled – reduced to the role of implementing other people's decisions and of dealing with their consequences. We have already considered the dangers of professional deskilling through the processes of increased managerialism. But this shows how professional deskilling can occur not just because of managerialism alone, but through a powerful combination of managerialism and organisational reactions to the emotional pressures of statutory work.

Perhaps the best way of coping with the emotional pressures is through containment. This is another psychodynamic concept, one developed by Wilfrid Bion (Symington and Symington, 1996). It describes the process by which, in Bion's original formulation, mothers 'take in' their baby's inchoate emotions, process and understand them, so that the baby can take back the now manageable feelings and gain the experience of having a 'containing' mother. In the organisational context, Hughes and Pengelly (1997) argue that containment is an important function of supervision; but making supervision work in this way requires a high degree of skill, as we shall see in Chapter 3.

FURTHER READING

Calder, M. (ed.) (2008) *The Carrot or the Stick? Towards Effective Practice with Involuntary Clients in Safeguarding Children Work*, Lyme Regis: Russell House Publishing. An edited collection of approaches to safeguarding children when they or their carers are 'involuntary clients'.
Trevithick, P. (2005) *Social Work Skills: A Practice Handbook* (2nd edn). Maidenhead: Oxford University Press. A thorough account of a wide range of social work skills that are applicable in all settings, not just in statutory contexts.
Trotter, C. (2006) *Working with Involuntary Clients: A Guide to Practice* (2nd edn). London: Sage. Describes an evidence-based approach to work with 'involuntary clients'.

Answers to Exercise 1.1

Appointment time	Sue	Mike
09.00	Call in at the local family centre to attend a review of a support package to a single parent: *Services to children in need are provided under s.17 of the Children Act 1989. The specific power to run family centres is in Schedule 2, s.9.*	Visit a couple at their home after their request for help in caring for their adult son, who has a learning disability: *Assessments of carers are carried out under the Carers (Recognition and Services) Act 1995.*

Appointment time	Sue	Mike
11.00	Attend a child protection case conference: *Arrangements for case conferences are in 'Working Together' (HM Government, 2006) guidance to local authorities issued under s.7 of the Local Authority Social Services Act 1970.*	Write a care plan: *Care planning takes place under the National Health Service and Community Care Act 1990.*
15.00	Make a home visit to arrange support for a young mother following her discharge from a mental hospital: *This could be done under s.117 of the Mental Health Act 1983 or under s.17 of the Children Act 1989.*	Discuss the provision of direct payments to a young woman who is deaf: *Direct payments for community care services can be made under the Health and Social Care Act 2001.*

2

Aims and Ethics

Chapter summary

This chapter is about the legitimacy of social work in statutory contexts. Should social workers be able to use the power of the state coercively? Could it be that compulsory admission to hospital for a mental health assessment, the use of care orders on children, or the supervision of reparation orders are examples of social workers using the power of the state to oppress disadvantaged people even further?

Arguments about the aims, values and legitimacy of social work in statutory contexts raise similar questions about social work as a whole. What is social work for, and what values does it hold? This chapter considers some of the possible answers to these big questions. It considers therapeutic views, social order views and transformational views of social work, before moving on to assess how they fit with the practice of such work in statutory contexts. Anti-oppressive practice is a key theme. Its principles of 'partnership', 'empowerment' and 'minimal intervention' present a particular challenge in statutory contexts. The chapter concludes with some ideas about how these challenges may be met.

Case example 2.1

Julie's social worker, Melanie, was in a state of shock. She sat rigid in her chair in a small meeting room as Julie paced the floor, circling round her, shouting and swearing, her face contorted with anger and sometimes thrust within inches of Julie's. 'You lot are all the same. They said I could have a new social worker – start again – but now it's another case conference and you are out to get this new baby as well. Well you are not taking it off me. . .'

Melanie had known that this was not going to be easy, but she had not expected this level of anger. This was her first meeting with Julie Morris, a pregnant 27-year old white English woman from a disadvantaged background. The new baby was due in six weeks' time. Julie's three previous children had been removed from her care and placed for adoption because of evidence of physical abuse and neglect. Julie had a history of being sexually abused as a child, of constantly running away from home and care placements, of self-harming and drug misuse and, as an adult, she had been diagnosed by a psychiatrist as having a personality disorder. Following discussions between the local authority and Julie's solicitors, it was agreed that Julie's relationship with her previous social worker had become so bad that the local authority would allocate a new social worker, Melanie Carter.

Melanie tried to explain that, because of the previous concerns, an initial child protection case conference was an inevitable part of the process, but that holding it did not imply that there was a plan automatically to take care proceedings or to seek the new baby's removal – either at birth or later. Unfortunately, such a long and complicated sentence was more than Melanie could manage under pressure, and her stumbling performance seemed only to enrage Julie even further. 'You don't know what you are talking about – I know you lot and I don't trust you an inch. You can't wait to get your hands on it. Well if anyone tries to take this one I'll kill them! Do you understand?'

As Julie continued to rant, Melanie began to think. Clearly her attempt to engage with Julie on a rational level, by explaining the logic of the child protection procedures, was not working. It was clear that Julie was extremely angry about the removal of her other children. Perhaps she had never had the chance to make this clear to anyone from the local authority? Perhaps allowing Julie to do so would somehow clear the air and pave the way for the new start that Julie was seeking? So Melanie sat still and listened, not defending her colleagues' earlier decisions, but gently declining to agree with Julie's assessment of them.

After an hour or so Julie began to calm down. Melanie undertook to show Julie, in advance, the report she would prepare for the case conference. Finally she was able to tell Julie that the intention was to support her and the new child together, probably in the context of a child protection plan, rather than to seek the baby's removal. There was an excellent local community support group that Julie could attend. Even when she was calmer, Julie continued to be angry about the prospect, claiming that the extra pressure of conferences and worrying about the baby's removal would be too much. She said that she would crack up under the pressure and then they would remove the baby anyway.

The Aims of Social Work

What is social work for? There is a variety of possible answers to this question. Payne (2006) has argued that there are three different groups of answers, which correspond broadly to three political views about social welfare. These are what he calls therapeutic views of social work; transformational views; and social order views.

Therapeutic views

Therapeutic views hold that the function of social work is to improve the well-being of individuals and groups by using insights into facilitating personal growth and individual fulfilment that come mainly from within the therapeutic tradition (for example Egan, 2006). On this view, in the course of their work social workers gain an increasing understanding of clients' perspectives, problems and ways to tackle them, and clients are influenced positively by workers. This fits with a social–democratic political philosophy of parallel economic and social development, which brings gains for individuals and society.

So, according to this view, Melanie's main objective in working with Julie would be to promote Julie's personal development, perhaps through counselling or through other broadly therapeutic approaches. Perhaps there is some evidence of Melanie beginning to work in this way, as she allows Julie to express some of her anger and gains a greater understanding of Julie's perspective.

Transformational views

Transformational views of social work are much more ambitious: they suggest 'that we must transform societies for the benefit of the poorest and most oppressed' (Payne, 2006: 13). Two arguments are most important. The first is that the nature of oppression and disadvantage means that people are unable to gain personal emancipation or empowerment without a radical transformation of society. The second is that traditional social work is complicit in the reproduction of oppression insofar as it assumes that individuals are responsible for their own difficult personal and social circumstances. Such arguments are sometimes described as 'critical', as they draw on a range of critical theory in sociology and beyond (for example Adams et al., 2002; Hick et al., 2005; Pease and Fook, 1999). They lead to forms of 'radical' or 'activist' social work practice (for example Fook, 1993; Healy, 1999). However, these forms of practice are themselves very diverse, as they include:

- anti-racist and multicultural social work
- anti-oppressive and anti-discriminatory social work
- feminist social work
- various strands of community work
- Marxist social work
- radical social work
- structural social work
- participatory and action forms of research. (Healy, 2000: 3)

Three important features are common to all these forms of practice. First, there is the expectation that social workers will not only reflect on their own access to power, but also find ways of sharing that power with service users (Dalrymple and Burke, 2006). Second, because dominant ideologies present the social order as natural and just, social workers must raise the consciousness of service users so that they come to understand how the causes of their difficulties lie in unjust social structures, and not in themselves (Mullaly, 2007). Finally, there is an emphasis on empowering service users to act collectively in agitating for social change. Such views broadly reflect a socialist political philosophy (Payne, 2006).

Applying these ideas to Melanie's work with Julie, we can identify ways in which Julie had experienced oppression and disadvantage. She had been brought up in a deprived area of the city and had been oppressed and sexually abused by her father. Taking a critical stance towards psychiatry, we might want to argue that the label of 'personality disorder' is an oppressive response to Julie's perhaps understandable reaction to these experiences. In the same vein, radical social work might question the social control inherent in the removal of three children from Julie's care (Corrigan and Leonard, 1978). Was this in any way a just response to Julie's difficulties? A transformational social work response would aim to empower Julie to overcome the impact of oppression, preferably alongside others. But if the oppression envisaged includes the possibility that the legal framework for child-care practice, the practice itself, or both, are unjust, then it is clear that there are some difficulties with practising radical social work within a statutory agency. Is social worker Melanie really in a position to side with Julie in criticising previous decisions taken by her own agency?

Social order views

Social order views bring these difficulties into sharp focus. Davies (1994) argues that social work is constrained by being party to the state's programme of social policy and practice. To put it bluntly, Davies argues that social workers are paid to follow the procedures of employing agencies and not to challenge the status quo. 'Maybe this is not what some people came into social work to do. If not, it is better for them to realize it early in their careers and to depart' (Davies, 1994: 116). In this less ambitious account of social work, the aim is to maintain the social order by helping people through any periods of difficulty, often so that they can recover and resume their social role. Davies (1994) calls these approaches 'maintenance approaches'. On this view, the aim of social work is not only to help service users, but also to help society by reconciling the two. As Payne (2006) argues, this expresses a liberal economic and political philosophy, based on personal freedom in the marketplace under the rule of law.

From this perspective, work with Julie would aim to support her to function as well as possible in the situation in which she found herself. This might involve a need to provide substantial services for her and for the new baby – perhaps practical, emotional and financial services, but always with the aim of withdrawing them once Julie would no longer require them.

Which view is the most accurate?

So: which of these views represents more closely what actually happens in social work practice? Payne (2006) argues that social work practice is a complex blend of all three perspectives. Depending on the context for practice and, sometimes, on the individual case, one or more of them may be more important. So, for example, an advocacy worker in a project dealing with domestic violence may have an important role in working for social change, whilst at the same time she may have a therapeutic role in relation to individuals. She is less likely to be interested in maintenance. On the other hand, the role of a worker in a youth offending team is primarily defined by concerns about maintaining social order, although she will also have an interest in working therapeutically with young people, and may also find limited ways of working to change the criminal justice system. So the answer is that the relative importance of the three perspectives depends on the practice setting. For our purposes, the question will be: which of these views of social work is the most relevant to statutory contexts? But before we can answer this question, we must first broaden the discussion to consider the values and the ethics of social work.

Exercise 2.1

Think of a particular example of social work that you have been involved in, or have read about. Which of the three views of social welfare (therapeutic, transformational, and social order) can you see reflected in the work? If more than one, then in what proportion?

Which of the three views seems the most important to you personally and what does this say about the kind of social work setting that you might wish to work in?

Social Work Values

How are these views about the purposes of social work related to the values and ethics of the profession? The word 'values' can be vague, as it has different meanings; but in current usage within social work it seems to refer to a 'whole range of beliefs about what is regarded as worthy or valuable in a social work context' (Banks, 2006: 6). This includes beliefs about the nature of a good society and about how to achieve it.

In his discussion of the value base of social work, Thompson (2005) divides social work values into two categories: traditional and emancipatory. We will examine each of these categories in turn and explore the linkages with the earlier discussion of the purposes of social work.

Traditional values

As the name implies, traditional values have been around since the early days of social work. In particular, the work of Biestek (1961) has been influential, and seven values that underpin the casework relationship are often cited. These are:

- *Individualisation* This value emerges from the need to recognise that people are unique individuals. Even when people appear to share a similar situation or set of difficulties, their precise circumstances will be unique and will have a specific meaning for each individual.

- *Purposeful expression of feelings* This value refers to the need to allow clients to express openly their feelings, especially the painful ones.

- *Controlled emotional involvement* This value encapsulates the need for workers to respond sensitively to clients' expressed feelings. It requires workers to be aware of their own feelings and neither to ignore them nor to become too emotionally involved.

- *Acceptance* This value expresses the need for workers to treat clients with dignity and respect, no matter who they are, what they may have done, and whether or not we like them. Human dignity and self worth are inherent in every individual and can neither be forfeited nor earned.

- *Non-judgemental attitude* This value is about the need to avoid making moral judgements about clients, particularly by approving or disapproving their behaviour, by finding them responsible for their problems, or by deciding whether or not they deserve help. (Note that being judgemental is very different from making professional judgements, despite the similarity of language. Professional judgement is based on evidence and analysis and is a vital element of good practice.)

- *Client self-determination* This value reflects the need to encourage clients to explore all the available options and to make their own decisions wherever possible. Limits to self-determination may be imposed by circumstances such as poverty, and sometimes by the worker's role in controlling client's behaviour, for example in youth justice.

- *Confidentiality* This is the right of clients to discuss sensitive, personal matters in private. However, Biestek does not present confidentiality as an absolute right. Disclosure of information amongst colleagues within the agency, in the context of supervision and support, has long been common practice. Disclosure between agencies is increasingly encouraged for the coordination of services. Concerns for the safety of others, particularly children, may also necessitate disclosure.

Traditional values place an emphasis on individuals and individual problems and, second, on aspects of the worker–client relationship as the site of change. Values such as acceptance, expression of feeling, and controlled emotional involvement are all firmly rooted in a therapeutic view of social work. However, in addition to this dominant therapeutic orientation, such traditional values also incorporate elements of the social order view. This is reflected in the recognition that the imperatives of social control which are inherent in social work place limits on client self-determination and on the right to confidentiality.

Emancipatory values

Emancipatory values are closely associated with transformational views of social work. Thompson (2005) identifies the following emancipatory values:

- *De-individualisation* This value names the need to understand that social forces shape the experiences of individuals, so that especially members of oppressed groups have much in common. Thompson argues that, despite appearances, this value is not in opposition to the traditional value of individualisation, but that the uniqueness of individuals can be valued at the same time as one understands the influence of broad social factors. As we will see, other writers choose to highlight the tensions between the two viewpoints.

- *Equality* This is not about treating everyone the same way, but rather about tackling inequality. What makes equality an emancipatory value is the fact that tackling inequality is not just about avoiding prejudice or discrimination in individual casework relationships (after all, this idea is inherent in traditional values) – it is about thinking and acting on power relationships at a structural level.

- *Social justice* This value refers to the need to try to combat poverty and social deprivation, not just to ignore it or collude with it.

- *Partnership* This is the need to work with clients and not to do things to them or for them.

- *Citizenship* The value given this name expresses the need to understand that clients have rights as citizens and that they are not just recipients of welfare. This fact is reflected in the change of language from 'client' to 'service user'. Above all, citizenship includes the right to participate in mainstream social life. Social work has the potential to add to the stigmatisation and social exclusion experienced by some service users or, through a focus on citizenship, to support the right to inclusion.

- *Empowerment* This is the need to help service users to gain greater control over their lives at interpersonal, social and political levels.

In assessing these values, it is clear that the notions of partnership and empowerment fit the transformational aim of attempting to share power with service users. Concern for social justice and equality draws attention to the ways in which the causes of their difficulties lie in unjust social structures. De-individualisation and citizenship point towards the possibilities of collective action. Taken as a whole, these emancipatory values coincide closely with a transformational view of social work.

Having considered various accounts of the general aims of social work and of the values associated with those aims, it is time to look more closely at social work in statutory contexts. Which of the three views of social work, with their associated values, is the most relevant in statutory contexts – or can we detect a combination of them?

The Goals and Values of Social Work in Statutory Contexts

As we saw in the previous chapter, the statutory basis of social work in England and Wales is contained in the Local Authority Social Services Act 1970 (LASSA). Schedule 1 to that Act lists each Act of Parliament that imposes a statutory function on local authorities, together with a brief account of these functions. That list is summarised in Table 1.1.

So, whatever the arguments may be over the purposes of social work in general, the statutory functions of local authorities are very clear and tightly defined. The remaining questions are:

- What kinds of social policy goals are reflected in this legislation?

- How do they tie in to the earlier discussion of the goals and values of social work?

Exercise 2.2

Consider the list of Acts of Parliament in Table 1.1. Select one related to an area of social work that interests you. Look particularly at the 'contents' page, to see the range of measures it contains. (This is available, along with the full text of the legislation, on the Office of Public Sector Information at www.opsi.gov.uk). Find and read any relevant commentaries about the aims and background of the legislation.

Which of the three aims of social work identified by Payne (2006) can you see reflected in the act? If more than one, then in what proportion?

A detailed analysis of the social policy context of all this legislation is well beyond the scope of this chapter. Other writers have given excellent accounts, for example in relation to the Children Act 1989 (Fox-Harding, 1991) and to the Mental Health Act 1983 (Rogers and Pilgrim, 2001). These writers point to the complexity of the underlying goals and to the ways in which legislation can often be seen as a compromise between the interests of different groups. Nonetheless, having looked at this list of legislation and compared it with the earlier accounts of the aims and values of social work, some fairly broad conclusions can be drawn.

First, the social work functions created by these acts reflect a primary concern for maintenance. This is hinted at by the very groups of people singled out for legal attention: children, older people, those with mental illness, disabled people. There is some overlap here with the concerns of transformational social work for oppressed or excluded groups, but black people, women, gay and lesbian people are noticeable by their absence from the statute. The primary concern for maintenance is perhaps confirmed by the fundamental requirement to provide services to support or to protect such people temporarily rather than to transform their social circumstances. Note that the legal requirement for protection introduces a secondary element of social control. Beckett and Maynard (2005) argue that the law regards social control as justified in three broad sets of circumstances:

- When individuals lack the understanding needed to take full responsibility for their own safety, the professional duty of care may extend to exercising some power over them.

- When individuals lack the power to protect themselves, social workers may have to exercise control over others.
- When individuals pose a threat to the public, social workers may have to exercise control over them.

Whilst it is certainly possible to see that some therapeutic goals are compatible with this primary agenda of maintenance and some social control, nonetheless there seems to be little evidence of any strongly transformational legislative purpose.

So perhaps we must conclude that social work in statutory contexts is restricted to a maintenance role, with some therapeutic possibilities. This certainly appears to be the position of Davies (1994), as quoted earlier. But his is a lonely voice, and the mainstream view continues to be that a commitment to the emancipatory values associated with social justice and social transformation is at the heart of social work in all its settings.

Since the late 1980s, the dominant expression of a commitment to a transformational view of social work in the UK has been through the concept of anti-oppressive practice. Writers such as Dalrymple and Burke (2006), Dominelli (1997) and Thompson (2006) have been influential in gaining international recognition for this approach. For a while, anti-oppressive practice was officially sanctioned by the Central Council for Education and Training in Social Work as the cornerstone of social work training in the UK (CCETSW, 1989), and it seems that the commitment to anti-oppressive practice in academic institutions remains strong (Thompson 2006).

Why has anti-oppressive practice proved so attractive? One explanation may be that it aims to unite the traditional values of individualisation with the transformational values of de-individualisation. It enables social workers to bring together critical perspectives arising from a structural critique of oppression (de-individualisation), and the traditional values of human uniqueness and individual experience (Horner, 2006: 101). We can have both. The claim is that individual casework may be practised anti-oppressively, by incorporating structural insights. Anti-oppressive practice recognises 'interpersonal and *statutory work* as legitimate sites of anti-oppressive practice' (Healy, 2005: 179, my italics).

The claim that anti-oppressive practice can be achieved in statutory contexts is important. As we have seen, on the face of it, the statutory functions of social work appear to fit with social order views, and perhaps with therapeutic views of social work – rather than with transformational views. So, if anti-oppressive practice brings together traditional and emancipatory values in ways that integrate the three views and can be practised in statutory contexts, then anti-oppressive practice is highly significant. The next section will first take a closer look at anti-oppressive practice and then examine its potential in statutory contexts.

Anti-Oppressive Practice

Anti-oppressive practice emerged from the broad genre of radical or critical approaches to social work, including anti-racist, feminist and structural approaches. In its own way, each of these is concerned with inequalities, marginalisation and disadvantage, but in the development of anti-oppressive practice these become central, generic and unifying concepts. In addition, anti-oppressive practice offers the chance to consider the interactions between different forms of oppression. In Julie's case above this would include poverty, educational disadvantage and the gendered experience of sexual abuse. Although there is no suggestion that any one form of oppression is any worse than another, nonetheless it is suggested that they add up, leading to double, triple or even quadruple oppression (Healy, 2000).

McDonald (2006) identifies some of the key themes of anti-oppressive practice.

- *Recognising social difference* means being alert to the influence of class, gender, race, religion, sexual preference, age, and disability.
- *Linking the personal and the political* means placing the experiences and life stories of individuals within a wider social context.
- *Working reflexively with mutual involvement* means understanding how values, social difference and power shape the interactions between people, including the relationships between social workers and service users. These relationships are to be understood not just in their psychological aspects, but also through the lens of sociology, history, politics and ethics.
- *Challenging for change* means creating opportunities at the individual and social level and linking theory and practice in the context of individual case stories.

Running through the literature on anti-oppressive practice are three major principles that we will consider in turn: empowering service users; working in partnership; and minimal intervention.

Empowering service users

'Addressing the ethics of empowerment in your work requires you to consider the power that you can exercise in relation to service users. It requires you to consider ways in which that power can be shared with and optimally transferred to the service user' (Parrott, 2006: 38).

This goal of sharing, or even transferring, the power of the social worker to the service user seems at first glance to be straightforward enough. However, as many commentators have observed, the concept of empowerment is problematic (Adams, 2003). Before we look at some of the problems most closely associated with statutory contexts in particular, here is a summary of some of the more general difficulties.

First, it has been argued that, because of focus on the techniques of empowering practice, there has been a general lack of clarity about the purposes of empowerment. For example, in relation to domestic violence, we might need to think carefully about which family members we were trying to empower: abusive father, abused mother or the children? As Fook puts it, 'we need to focus on the harder questions like empowerment for what and for whom?' (2002: 8). Second, service users may have the paradoxical experience of empowerment done to them by others (Parker et al., 1999). If service users are passively in receipt of empowerment, then we must question whether the latter is actually being achieved. A related danger is that of a professional colonisation of the concept of empowerment (Wilson and Beresford, 2000), such that either empowerment becomes tokenistic and there is no change in the pattern of service delivery, or consumerist ideologies take hold (Adams, 2003).

Some writers are pessimistic. Dominelli argues that empowerment is 'unable to do more than deal with issues at the micro-level of practice in the practitioner–client relationship, and has little impact on structural inequalities' (2004: 63). Others, such as Mullaly (2007), argue that structural empowerment is achievable, even if this means the development of alternative services and organisations outside the statutory sector. However, it may be that postmodern insights into the nature of power itself are changing the terms of this debate and are suggesting new possibilities for anti-oppressive practice, as we will see later in this chapter.

Working in partnership

The idea here is that 'service users must be included as far as possible as citizens in the decision-making processes which affect their lives' (Dalrymple and Burke, 2006: 132–3). But it is acknowledged explicitly that genuine partnerships are difficult to achieve, precisely because of the unequal power relationships that give rise to the need for an empowering practice. These relationships are rooted in the stigma attached to using social work services, the vested power interests of professionals and service providers, agency accountability to funding bodies rather than to service users, and the social control functions of social work in statutory contexts (Healy, 2005). The latter point is one we will return to when assessing the potential for anti-oppressive practice in statutory contexts.

Accepting the reality of unequal power relationships in child protection work, Thorburn and colleagues (1995) introduced the idea of a ladder. This was first developed to describe the involvement of citizens in planning processes in the US. The bottom rung represents the manipulation of citizens by professionals. The second rung represents placation, followed by informing, consultation, involvement, participation, partnership and, finally, the delegation of power. This is clearly a hierarchy, and it makes the implication that the delegation of power is an ideal. A similar hierarchy was adopted in influential official child protection guidance in the same year (Department of Health, 1995b). There has been considerable debate about the usefulness of this concept in statutory contexts, and there is evidence from research that partnership is not achieved very much in child-care practice (see for example Bell, 1996; Bell, 1999; Corby et al., 1996; Healy, 1998).

Minimal intervention

This is another response to the unequal power relationships between social workers and service users. Here the aim is to intervene in the least intrusive and least oppressive way possible (Dalrymple and Burke, 2006; Healy, 2005). Minimal intervention is an argument for placing the emphasis on the kinds of services that might prevent social problems, rather than on those that respond once something has gone wrong. This is because preventive services can be user-led, non-stigmatising and open to all, whereas intervention in response to specific concerns tends to be much more intrusive (Parrott, 2006). The underlying principle is that 'intervention should only be either at the request of the service user, or on the basis of a clear statutory mandate' (Beckett and Maynard, 2005: 164–5). And when the intervention comes in response to a statutory mandate, then it is argued that the principle of minimal intervention is more important than ever, because of the following dangers:

- Frequent use of statutory powers may easily desensitise us to the seriousness of them.
- The fact that we can resort to these powers may tempt us to do so, even in situations which could in fact be resolved, given time, by negotiation and mutual agreement.
- The more that statutory powers are used, the greater the potential for social workers to become objects of fear in the communities where they work, thus eroding the trust that is required if they are to be able to work in supportive and non-threatening ways.
- Statutory powers can be abused to meet our own needs: to allay our own fears of losing control, for instance, or even to 'punish' a service user we have experienced as difficult. (Beckett and Maynard, 2005: 120)

Links to practice

Let us return to the case of Julie Morris and consider the intervention that has occurred so far in the light of the principles of anti-oppressive practice. First, we might argue that the provision of a new social worker, Melanie, could be seen as an attempt to empower Julie by offering her the opportunity of a fresh start. Melanie's commitment to listening to Julie's anger could be seen not only through a therapeutic lens, as we saw it before, but also as an attempt to lay the grounds for some sort of meaningful partnership with her. And the principle of minimal intervention could be seen reflected in the plan to support Julie and the new baby rather than in any plan to seek legal powers to remove the child.

Yet some might argue that this hardly does justice to the ideals of anti-oppressive practice. Where is the challenge for social change at a structural level? As we noted earlier, Melanie might be aware of the multiple oppressions that Julie has experienced; but how can this affect her practice? Three children have already been removed from Julie through legal action, and this is why she is angry and mistrustful. Despite her being aware of these multiple oppressions, there is no suggestion that Melanie has questioned whether removing the children was the right thing to do. Should she have done so? Perhaps Dominelli (2004) is right to claim than an anti-oppressive approach to individual casework cannot challenge large-scale structural inequalities? In the next section we will assess the potential for anti-oppressive practice in statutory contexts and, in doing so, we will tackle these questions directly.

Anti-Oppressive Practice in Statutory Contexts

The primary functions of social work practice in statutory contexts are tightly defined by the law. But this is not to argue that the law is always clear, or that its application is always straightforward. Braye and Preston-Shoot (1997) argue that the law contains within itself competing imperatives, for example in relation to needs versus rights, welfare versus justice, and individual autonomy versus social control. This means that the law may not provide clarity for social workers about exactly when and how to intervene. This is left rather to the judgement and professionalism of the practitioner (Thompson, 2005).

The law does not solve our practice dilemmas, although it defines their parameters. For example, the concept of significant harm is central to the operation of the Children Act 1989 in England and Wales, and harm is defined in s.31 (9) as 'ill-treatment or the impairment of health or development'. But the legislation makes no attempt to define the term 'significant'. This is deliberate. Significance is judged and defined in practice, by practitioners and courts, in individual cases. The fact that the law is not totally prescriptive means that there is certainly room for social workers to exercise considerable discretion. However, the question that we must now address is whether or not it is possible to practise anti-oppressively in statutory contexts.

Strengths and limitations

In statutory contexts there is a tendency for social work to become individualised at the level of cases. One of the strengths of anti-oppressive practice is that it places social justice centre stage, not blaming individuals for their own problems but recognising the personal, cultural and structural elements of oppression. By emphasising structural elements, anti-oppressive practice claims its roots in the transformational views of social work. However, the focus on local elements of practice and on the nature of the relationship between social worker and service user means that, whilst espousing these more ambitious, transformational goals, anti-oppressive practice is able to occupy some of the territory shared by therapeutic views of social work. All this is positive.

Yet there are serious limitations, particularly in relation to work in statutory contexts. One significant aspect of such work is the need to manage high-risk cases, where death or serious injury are possible outcomes. As Healy (2005) argues, when one works in mental health or child protection, individual psychological factors may be a key to understanding and managing risk. But the strong critique of therapeutic views and of the psychological approaches that underpin them, together with the preference for a structural analysis of oppression, may lead anti-oppressive practitioners away from the appropriate intervention in high-risk cases. This tendency may be reinforced by the emphasis on minimal intervention. As we have seen, part of the rationale for minimising intervention is supplied by an understanding of the dangers of statutory interventions.

But the exercise of power in social work may have positive benefits, and may even be experienced as helpful. In the context of child protection, a more sophisticated view of power relations within families may challenge the assumption that those who are subjected to statutory power will always experience power as coercive. The imposition of control over one member of the family may provide a way out of an untenable situation for another member. We should acknowledge 'the potentially productive effects of statutory power, particularly in relation to the protection of those family members who are most vulnerable to abuse' (Healy, 1998: 909). This is to begin to prioritise the conflicting needs of different service users, even within the same family, in a way that is not suggested by anti-oppressive practice. We are beginning to address Fook's question – empowerment 'for what and for whom?' (2002: 8).

The argument here is that the statutory context for much of social work is, at best, an uneasy fit with some of the central ideas of anti-oppressive practice. This is contrary to the claim of some anti-oppressive practice theorists. They might argue that one of the features that distinguish anti-oppressive practice from other transformational approaches is precisely its applicability to casework and to statutory contexts. But, as we have seen, empowerment may seem counterproductive in situations where the aim is to control abusive behaviour. Partnership may be impossible where there is no agreement whatsoever over the goals of the intervention. And minimal intervention carries with it the danger of failing to manage risk adequately.

So: are there any other ways of thinking about statutory work and anti-oppressive practice that might help to resolve some of these dilemmas? Recently there has been a growing interest in the application of postmodern thinking to social work. Whilst there is no suggestion here that postmodernism 'solves' these problems, nonetheless there are several features of postmodern thinking that appear to be highly relevant to work in statutory contexts. First, postmodern theorists have begun to develop a more sophisticated approach to understanding the operation of power. Second, there is an emphasis on deconstructing binary opposites, such as care and control. Finally, there is an emphasis on the local and the contextual that may open the way to a more detailed understanding of practice. The following section describes some of these features.

The Influence of Postmodernism

The exercise of power

By now it should be clear that questions about power are at the heart of social work in statutory contexts. Yet power is a very complex concept and postmodern approaches to power are diverse. This section gives a very brief summary of how some of the ideas of the influential French philosopher Michel Foucault may be relevant to social work in statutory contexts.

Foucault's approach to power rejects the 'juridico-discursive' model, which understands power as belonging to, or being inherent in, some individuals and imposed on others. In Foucault's view, power is not a commodity, but rather it is an ever present feature of social relations, an inescapable part of daily life. Furthermore, it is productive as well as it is repressive, insofar as submission to 'disciplinary power' (for example, dietary and fitness regimes) confers a positive sense of identity, gives pleasure and enhances the capacities of individuals. Whilst not denying the existence of oppressive social structures such as capitalism and patriarchy, Foucault's approach does not accept that these are the *cause* of an individual's local experiences of oppression. Instead, the logic runs the other way: global structures are built on the back of accumulated local experience. These three points can be summarised as follows:

- Power is exercised, not possessed.
- Power is both repressive and productive.
- Power comes from the bottom up. (Healy, 2005: 52)

What are the implications of these ideas for social work in statutory contexts? First, if power is not a commodity that is possessed, then it cannot be simply shared with, or transferred to, service users. We need to rethink our concept of empowerment. Second, if power is also exercised by relatively powerless individuals and groups, albeit in covert or limited ways, then this has several implications. It means that, in any situation where the statutory function leads social workers to attempt to change or control aspects of a service user's behaviour, they should expect resistance (Harris, 1997). On the other hand, it means that there may be previously unimagined opportunities to support the capacities of abused children – for example as they exercise some power in resistance. Finally, if power is both repressive and productive, then the exercise of power at a local level becomes more complex and contradictory than might be apparent at a global level (Fook, 2002).

So a mother such as Julie in our example may be relatively powerless in relation to her abusive father or to the social services department, but she may be relatively powerful in relation to her children (Featherstone and Fawcett, 1994). In the same way, the social worker Melanie may be relatively powerful in relation to Julie but feel relatively powerless in the face of the bureaucracy in which she works. And the relative positions of power in the relationship between them may change as they negotiate over the nature of the proposed services to support Julie. Julie may refuse to accept, for example, Melanie's suggestion that she might attend a community support group; and in the end some acceptance of the need for support is essential if the plan is to work. So the skills of negotiation and persuasion are important, as we will see in later chapters, but they are played out in the context of complex and fluid local power dynamics involving the service user, the social worker and the worker's employing agency. Social workers need to be aware of these dynamics and of their own part in them if they are to recognise and support service users in the appropriate exercise of power. In other words, they need to be both critical and reflective in their approach to empowerment (Fook, 1999).

Questioning categories of opposites

Postmodernists are highly suspicious of fixed binary distinctions between categories of opposites. Yet the identities of social workers and service users in relation to each other are often constituted around dualistic categories such as:

- middle class/working class;
- privileged/poor;
- technical knowledge/lived experience;
- voice/silence;
- researcher/researched;
- worker/service user;
- powerful/powerless. (Healy, 1999: 122)

Postmodernists accept that significant differences of these types exist, but they note the negative consequences of constructing them as mutually exclusive opposites. The argument is that these dualisms mask significant differences within categories, significant similarities between apparently opposed categories, and the significance of changes in status over time. By recognising, for example, the differences in the experiences of individual women or disabled people, we can reach an understanding that is more rooted in the local context of individual lives, and therefore of greater relevance to social work practice. Similarities between categories, for example between social workers and service users, are also important. Experience as a service user is a fairly common motivation for becoming a social worker, and one that is often overlooked. In addition, workers and service users often share a sense of identity as parents – or perhaps as employees – that may be significant in shaping the work.

In statutory contexts, a significant binary distinction is often made between care and control. In her account of social work skills, Trevithick, for example, writes about the need to balance 'the conflicting demands of care and control' (2005: 218). Beckett and Maynard (2005), whilst not adopting an explicitly postmodern stance, argue that care and control are not necessarily in conflict at all. In situations where individuals lack understanding or power, a professional duty of care may necessarily include elements of control. '"Control", used appropriately, is not the opposite of care, but on the contrary is an expression of care' (Beckett and Maynard, 2005: 120).

The local and contextual

Postmodern insights suggest that local and contextual factors may be more significant than anti-oppressive practice theorists have previously thought. For example, whereas Burke and Harrison argue that '[a] white male social worker brings to the situation a dynamic that will reproduce the patterns of oppression to which black women are subjected in the wider society' (2002: 232), Healy (2005) takes issue with this, arguing that membership of a particular group (white male social worker) is not enough to account for local power relations. Other factors, such as the philosophy of his employing agency, the legislative context of the work, and his own value positions and those of the black woman he is working with will have a substantial effect on the outcome.

Incorporating postmodern insights

Many radical social workers are sceptical about the contribution of postmodern insights. There are real political dangers in undermining the group identities in relation to class, gender or disability, which support collective action (Dominelli, 2002; Ife, 1999). There is also concern that losing the certainties and identities of modern critical social theories means that activists are left high and dry.

So the argument here is not that we should adopt postmodern ways of thinking instead of alternatives. As Ife (1999) argues, post-modernism is not an all-or-nothing choice for social workers. The ability of postmodern theorists to deconstruct binary opposites is relevant here. As Fook and Pease put it:

> We believe that one of the difficulties in accepting postmodern thinking lies in the modernist assumption that theoretical positions are mutually exclusive, implying that one can have allegiance to only one at a time. It is our contention that postmodern thinking does not attempt to posit one underlying causal explanation for phenomena. Thus there is no logical reason why aspects of postmodern thinking cannot sit easily with other causal theories, since it does not seek to replace other explanations, but rather to make observations about our process of deriving explanations. (Fook and Pease, 1999: 228)

The challenge is to find ways of integrating postmodern insights so as to address some of the identified limitations of anti-oppressive practice in statutory contexts. This is a challenge that runs right through this book.

Conclusion

Although there are some difficulties with applying the principles of anti-oppressive practice to social work in statutory settings, nonethe-less we should not abandon this approach. We should not accept that social work in statutory contexts is limited to social control and maintenance, controlling the behaviour of some individuals and helping others to cope with difficult and unjust circumstances, although these functions are both important and legitimate. In order to fit with the emancipatory values of social work as a whole, social work in statutory contexts should also be about social justice. We should understand that discrimination, disadvantage and exclusion underlie many of the problems addressed in statutory contexts. We need to retain a critical approach to the legal framework and the impact of social work in statutory contexts. But, insofar as we accept the aims and legitimacy of the legal framework for our interventions, we also need to be realistic about the extent to which any meaningful transformation of society is possible as a result of such work. As we have seen, statutory contexts are not a natural fit with transformational forms of social work. If we believe in the value of social work in statutory contexts, then the challenge is to find ways of working anti-oppressively whilst not losing sight of the fact that the legitimate aims of the intervention may involve exercising control over others.

The second half of the book takes up this challenge in the context of specific skills. Some possible strategies have already been identified – for example, by being clear about the aims of our interventions (who for and why?), by developing a more sophisticated approach to understanding the operation of power, by deconstructing binary opposites and by emphasising the local and the contextual. But it should be acknowledged that these conceptual ideas are a long way removed from the concrete realities of practice. Individual social workers have much critical thinking to do before they can figure out what anti-oppressive practice might look like in any individual case. What follows in the second half of the book is an attempt to help with this process.

FURTHER READING

Banks, S. (2006) *Ethics and Values in Social Work*, 3rd edn. Basingstoke: Palgrave Macmillan. Includes an account of the ethical basis of radical/ emancipatory and postmodern approaches to social work.
Davies, M. (1994) *The Essential Social Worker*, 3rd edn. Aldershot: Arena. Davies argues that the 'maintenance' theory best explains the role of social work in society.
Healy, K. (2000) *Social Work Practices: Contemporary Perspectives on Change*. London: Sage. A stimulating account of critical perspectives in social work and of their relationship to debates about postmodernism.

Payne, M. (2006) *What Is Professional Social Work?* 2nd edn. Bristol: Policy Press. A classic analysis of three views of social work: therapeutic, transformational and social order.

Thompson, N. (2006) *Anti-Discriminatory Practice*, 4th edn. Basingstoke: Palgrave Macmillan. A very readable introduction to anti-discriminatory practice in social work.

Part II
Skills

3

Skills for Working in Organisations

Chapter summary

This chapter considers the skills that social workers require in order to work within organisations that have statutory social work powers and duties. These include the generic skills associated with supervision and the use of procedures, but they are considered here in the light of the specific pressures identified in Chapter 1 on organisations that have statutory duties. The chapter is concerned with the relationships between social workers and their managers, particularly with the power dynamics. It considers the skills that social workers use to work confidently and constructively with their managers in statutory contexts in the interests of those to whom they have a statutory duty.

Skills for Making Use of Supervision

In statutory contexts, the relevant legal powers and duties lie with public bodies. Social workers are employed to carry out these duties on behalf of the statutory organisation. Supervision is where individual social workers and their managers meet to consider the work being undertaken. It represents the interface between the professional practice of the individual social worker and the requirements of the organisation. It might seem obvious that a cooperative relationship between the two is the ideal, but nonetheless a critical understanding of the power dynamics of this relationship is essential if we are to work towards achieving it in the context of an employer/employee relationship. It is a two-way process, and consequently there should be nothing passive about being supervised. This is not something that is done to you as a social worker. On the contrary, social workers need to draw on a range of skills in order to make supervision work effectively. But talk of effective supervision means that we should in the first place look more carefully at the dynamics of supervision and at the critical questions of whom and what supervision is for.

Aims of supervision

Supervision has been an integral part of social work practice from its earliest days. Conceptually it is complex because, although it is usually a meeting of only two people – supervisor and social worker – it involves four parties: the employing agency, the supervisor, the social worker and the service user (Tsui, 2005). At a fundamental level, the four parties may have a common interest in using supervision to support high-quality social work services. But, as we have seen in Chapter 2, in statutory contexts social workers and service users may not be working in straightforwardly cooperative partnerships, and the different parties have different interests too. Agencies want staff to carry out agency policy and procedure; line managers want to ensure that social workers are using their time effectively; and social workers may want various kinds of support for their work. In statutory social work contexts the supervisor is usually also the social worker's line manager, and thus also represents the agency's interests. Service users' interests are represented only indirectly.

Morrison (2001) lists four functions of supervision, as follows:

- the managerial (normative) function
- the educative (formative) function
- the supportive (restorative) function
- the mediation function.

These four functions do not have a direct one-to-one correlation with the interests of the four parties identified by Tsui (2005). It may be helpful to explore the relationships between the four functions and the interests of the four parties.

The managerial function is designed to ensure that the worker is doing the job properly, in line with the agency's standards and procedures. The supervisor will monitor standards and, at the same time, help the worker to understand what is expected of her. The managerial function consists primarily in looking after the interests of super-visor and employing agency – but, of course, workers and service users have an interest in this too. The managerial function is where the relative power of the employer is at its most clear.

The educative function is designed to help workers to develop their levels of skills. The supervisor will help the worker to learn from their practice through critical reflection (Karvinen-Niinikoski, 2004) and to identify training needs. This objective is primarily directed at meeting the needs of workers; but, again, the other parties also have an interest it.

The supportive function is described by Morrison (2001) as a safe, trusting relationship, in which the worker can deal with the personal impact of the work. Morrison's description of the supportive super-visory relationship draws on the concept of containment (see Chapter 1) and includes permission to talk about feelings and work stresses. Once again, this function is primarily intended to meet the needs of workers. However, as we saw earlier, the emotional impact of statutory work is not confined to individual workers but also affects organisations. We should not see it just as a personal problem for individual workers.

Finally, the mediation function is meant to facilitate communica-tion between worker and organisation. The supervisor will brief the worker about organisational developments and the worker will report on practice issues, including resource deficits. The assumption is that this is a two-way process of mutual benefit. However, in the context of rapidly evolving organisations, significant resource shortages and increasing managerialism, this is one of the functions of supervision that can lead to tensions in the relationship and consequently may be avoided.

Morrison (2001) argues that the ideal situation is one in which these four functions of supervision are held in balance, none taking priority over the others. Yet, as we have seen, the pressures of accountability in statutory work, combined with the impact of mana-gerialism and the emotional stress, mean that there is a strong ten-dency for the managerial function to override the other three. This is certainly the experience of workers in Banks' (2004) study. When this happens, supervision may be experienced as oppressive, and the opportunities for creative work with service users, always elusive in statutory contexts, become even harder to find. So an important skill for making use of supervision in statutory contexts is to ensure that the four functions are kept in balance.

Skill summary: Balancing the four functions of supervision

This is not the sole responsibility of the social worker but is shared with the supervisor. Social workers must be active alongside their supervisors in order to maintain the balance.
Strategies include:

- discussing the purposes of supervision with your supervisor at an early stage
- making sure that written contracts for supervision acknowledge the significance of all four functions
- agreeing on an agenda for individual supervision sessions that allocates time for each
- keeping an audit on supervision records of time spent on each
- agreeing that any dissatisfaction with the balance is an important topic for discussion in itself.

Learning this skill will help you to meet the following National Occupational Standards:

Key Role 5: Unit 14.

What to expect from supervision

Expectations from supervision can be vague unless they are formally recorded. Contracts are a very useful way of doing this. Although some may resent the creation of yet more paperwork, nonetheless there are powerful arguments in favour of written supervision contracts:

- Contracts reflect the importance of supervision.
- Most difficulties in supervision stem from a lack of clarity about authority and accountability. Reliance on verbal agreements can exacerbate this.
- Written contracts define both parties' responsibilities, thus emphasising the active role of the supervisee.
- Written contracts are open to review and to audit.
- Negotiating a contract in a context of differing roles, power and authority is a good model for statutory work with service users (Morrison, 2001).

Supervision contracts should be negotiated, not imposed. Nonetheless, contracts should make clear those elements of agency policy and procedure that are not normally negotiable in a statutory agency – for example the requirement to hold regular supervision, or the responsibilities and powers of line managers. They should clarify the limits of confidentiality, including arrangements for recording supervisions and the uses that may be made of records. In statutory work there is also a need to be clear about the relationship between those key case management decisions that may be taken in supervision and those that may be taken in other meetings. For example, worker and supervisor might agree in supervision that a looked-after child should be moved from one foster carer to another, but any formal decision would usually be taken in a review meeting involving other people. Contracts should also make clear the workers' requirement for support and personal development and should have an agreed way of dealing with some of the interpersonal issues in supervision that can block progress.

Negotiation over supervision contracts can be seen to mirror the kinds of negotiation over planned interventions that take place with service users in statutory contexts. In both situations there is a need for clarity about which elements of the relationship are negotiable and which are imposed by the statutory context – in other words, about the context for the power dynamics. Being thoughtful and careful in setting up the detail of supervision contracts can act as excellent preparation for undertaking similar exercises with service users.

Working with feelings in supervision

Case example 3.1

Social worker James, who is white, takes seven-year-old Malik to see his mother, Rasheeda. Both are British Muslims and their family is of Pakistani origin. Rasheeda was compulsorily admitted to hospital in England under the Mental Health Act 1983 by another social worker, three months ago, after she stabbed Malik in the back during what the psychiatrist described as a psychotic episode. Malik was not seriously injured, but the intake and assessment team of the local authority has started care proceedings and an interim care order has been granted. Malik is living with foster carers. The case has recently been transferred to James, who works with looked-after children.

James has spent time with Malik and understands that the latter is confused and hurt. James also believes that Malik is desperate to see Rasheeda, and so the visit has been arranged. But nothing prepared James for the reality. The hospital is grim and does not have adequate facilities for children. The meeting takes place in a small meeting room with a window on to a busy corridor. Rasheeda is completely overcome with emotion and cries throughout. Malik has brought a card and a gift but, if Rasheeda notices at all, then it just makes her even more upset. Malik is calm and stoical, showing little feeling. There is little communication between the parties. Afterwards, having taken Malik back to the foster carers, James has a sense of overwhelming sadness and hopelessness about the situation, combined with guilt and some anger with having exposed Malik to this experience.

In this case example, James is left with some very strong feelings that he must find a way to cope with. One strategy is to use supervision as a place where those feelings can be recognised, validated and contained. This has a clear benefit for James. But it may also help Malik. As James has felt very bad after the visit, there is a danger that he may react by distancing himself from Malik. He might delay his next visit, or he may fail to plan another meeting between Malik and Rasheeda. Arguably neither of these reactions would be helpful. Talking about his feelings in supervision may help James to cope with them and thus it may lead to better decisions about what to do next.

But using supervision in this way takes skill and some courage, not least because it is sensible to be cautious about exposing what might be interpreted as weakness in the context of an employer/employee relationship. Confidence that a supervisor will respond appropriately is something which is often built up in steps, over a period of time.

Skill summary: Using supervision to help in coping with intense emotions

Whilst it is true that supervisors play a part in giving permission for the expression of feelings and in responding skilfully to it, nonetheless they cannot be expected to know exactly when the worker is experiencing strong emotions and needs to talk about them. Consequently workers need to be active in order to gain the support they need.
Strategies include:

- keeping some form of reflective diary that includes feelings
- challenging the idea that experiencing difficult feelings is a sign of weakness or incompetence

- normalising the discussion of feelings in supervision as an integral part of the work
- recognising that additional stress-management techniques may also be needed.

Learning this skill will help you to meet the following National Occupational Standards:

Key Role 5: Unit 14.

So far we have treated feelings generated by the work as a pressure that needs to be coped with. However, there is another way of looking at feelings. From a psychodynamic perspective, they can be seen as giving clues about the experience of service users (Hughes and Pengelly, 1997).

In our example, James' feelings of sadness, hopelessness, anger and guilt may be a reflection of how Malik is feeling and may help him and his supervisor to understand Malik's position. But, clearly, in considering how much weight to give to workers' feelings as evidence about a service user's experience, we need to understand the workers' state of mind. Are these feelings just about Malik, or is there anything else that might be adding to James' feelings of sadness? For this reason, James and his supervisor may sometimes need to talk about issues in James' life that are not directly related to his work.

In psychodynamic terms, *transference* is the process by which Malik unconsciously projects his sad feelings about his mother onto his relationship with his social worker, James. And *countertransference* is the process in which feelings, thoughts and, sometimes, behaviours are stimulated in James in response to Malik's transference. Going one step further, psychodynamic theorists suggest that sometimes the dynamics of the original relationship are *mirrored* in the supervisory relationship (Mattinson, 1975). In the case under discussion, it is possible that Malik's anger with his mother, experienced by James through countertransference, is being played out as James feels angry with his supervisor as a representative of the agency that was responsible for the compulsory admission to hospital, or for the poor state of facilities for visiting children.

Working in supervision with the complexity of these dynamic processes is a skilled task. Critics have argued that using these ideas to explain difficult feelings or behaviour in professionals is simply another way of blaming service users, since this manner of thinking sees them and their experiences as the original source of the difficulty.

Clearly there is a real danger of this happening, and such danger may be exacerbated by the intense pressure, in statutory work, to justify and account for professional actions. We need to take a critical stance, always questioning the way in which power relationships affect practice and trying to identify whose interests are being served. But, in supervision, thoughtful attention to the dynamics that underpin workers' feelings can provide a useful source of information about the progress of the work itself.

Skill summary: Using feelings in supervision to help to progress the work

Talking about the feelings that the work is generating for the worker can provide valuable insights into the position of service users and into the impact of interventions. It can be helpful in making assessments and in planning interventions. It may also help staff to understand difficulties in the supervisory relationship. Skilled work in this area will include:

- awareness of feelings generated and willingness to talk about them
- a grounding in relevant psychodynamic concepts
- awareness of the potential for oppressive practice if service users are 'blamed'.

Learning this skill will help you to meet the following National Occupational Standards:

Key Role 2: Unit 5.
Key Role 5: Unit 14.

Getting the most from supervision

In our example, James is confused about what his experience of visiting the hospital with Malik means. Does the fact that Malik appeared calm and stoical whilst James felt both sad and angry indicate anything about the value of continued contact? Is the experience so upsetting for Malik that it might be better for him not to continue to see his mother? Should he wait until she has recovered? Or, James wonders, does this thought reflect just his own desire to protect Malik (and himself) from a difficult situation?

In preparation for supervision, James realises that the two issues – the question of what to do about future contact and the feelings he experienced – are inextricably linked together. His approach is to write down some of the relevant feelings and issues in advance and to put them on the agenda for supervision.

Skill summary: Preparing for supervision

It is the social worker's responsibility to bring important issues to supervision. These may include case management issues (what to do next and how), issues arising from feelings generated, and reflections on the work, including lessons learnt. Skilled preparation may include:

- reviewing case records as needed
- keeping and consulting a reflective diary.

Learning this skill will help you to meet the following National Occupational Standards:

Key Role 1: Unit 1.
Key Role 5: Unit 14.

In the resulting session, James suspects that his supervisor may be critical of the fact that he had not adequately checked the hospital's visiting arrangements for children. He is feeling bad about it himself. But was there anything more that he could have done? After all, he doesn't run the hospital. James is keen to know what his supervisor thinks.

Skill summary: Receiving and giving feedback about performance

In statutory work fear of criticism can be a significant dynamic. Workers need to give permission for feedback, preferably in the supervision contract. Skills in giving feedback include making it:

- specific and focused on things that can be changed
- balanced – awarding praise and criticism as appropriate
- planned – not a spontaneous outburst!
- owned by the supervisor ('my observations of you are . . .').

Workers should expect to give feedback to supervisors on their own performance.

> Learning this skill will help you to meet the following National Occupational Standards:
>
> Key Role 5: Unit 14.
> Key Role 6: Unit 19.

In fact James' supervisor appears to be distracted. She has turned up late and James feels that she doesn't seem to understand his dilemma. And this is not the first time that James has felt this way in supervision. What should he do?

Skill Summary: Dealing with difficulties in supervision

Some level of difficulty in supervision needs to be regarded as routine. At the very least, from time to time boredom and dissatisfaction will creep in. In the statutory context, fear of blame and heightened emotion add to the difficulties. Skills in dealing with difficulties include:

- a specific commitment to being open about these issues – preferably in the supervision agreement
- normalising these issues.

Learning this skill will help you to meet the following National Occupational Standards:

Key Role 5: Unit 14.
Key Role 6: Unit 19.

Skills for Using Procedures

We have seen how, in statutory social work, the twin pressures of accountability and difficult emotional content add to the managerial tendency towards a procedure-driven practice. Since the 1980s, when child protection procedures were first introduced in the UK as a response to findings of public inquiries, statutory social work agencies have also introduced detailed procedures in most other areas of their work. Procedures can outline the specific actions that the worker must take (for example, whom to invite or when to set up a child protection case conference); or they can be forms that must be filled in (for example in completing a community care assessment); and, very often, they include both.

There are potential benefits here. Procedures can bring clarity and focus to the task. By making decision-making processes and criteria transparent they can promote equity in access to services, enhance accountability and uphold the rights of service users. On the other hand, there are complaints about a proliferation of procedures to such an extent that workers lose track of them, and they are ignored. Perhaps even more fundamentally, there is concern that procedures are too prescriptive and that completing check boxes leads to a deskilled, reductionist version of social work (Dominelli, 2004). As we have seen, workers in Banks' (2004) study complained that they were no longer able to respond to service users as whole people, by responding flexibly to needs – including emotional ones. Instead they had to work through lists of predetermined questions, some of which seemed irrelevant, or even disrespectful. This kind of social work appeared to be the very antithesis of the one that had motivated them to enter the profession in the first place.

Advocates of procedures sometimes defend them by claiming that they are not necessarily as prescriptive as they appear, but are intended to provide a framework for practice in which workers maintain room for manoeuvre. Consider the following case example.

Case example 3.2

Jane has a problem. She is a social worker visiting Mrs Stephenson for the first time in order to carry out a community care assessment. Mrs Stephenson is a white woman aged 76. She lives alone and has recently been discharged from hospital. The procedure involves a long list of questions that Jane must obtain answers to in order to establish both need and eligibility. Jane has explained both the purpose of the visit and the process, but Mrs Stephenson is not in the mood to answer Jane's questions and keeps changing the subject. She wants to tell Jane about her relationship with her sister, which is bad as a consequence of a row during the previous week. She also has a lot to tell Jane about her recent hospital admission. Both matters have been seriously upsetting to her. The problem for Jane is how to work through the checklist of questions without alienating Mrs Stephenson and projecting an image of herself as an officious bureaucrat.

A solution occurs to Jane when she realises that the topics are actually related. Mrs Stephenson's sister had been providing some care, and much of Mrs Stephenson's talk about the hospital is also about her care needs.

Jane finds that she is able to link some of the questions on her list (for example the ones about support from family members) to the topics that Mrs Stephenson is talking to her about. Over the next few minutes Jane pays careful and empathic attention to Mrs Stephenson's story, making sensitive links to relevant questions where these suggest themselves. At the end of this phase, Jane has gained much relevant information and, more importantly, Mrs Stephenson feels that she has been listened to and is now much more willing to return to the remainder of Jane's questions.

Following or using procedures?

In the example above, Jane understands the relevance of the information that the procedure requires her to collect. In fact, by the end of the interview she has collected it, without ever having followed the sequence of questions on the assessment form and without having allowed the form to dictate the shape of the interview. On the contrary, she has been able to respond in the first place to Mrs Stephenson's agenda for the interview and to tune in to the particularity of her needs and to her individual situation.

Underlying this discussion about procedures are the big questions raised earlier about what motivates social workers to do statutory work. You will notice that Jane wanted to present herself to Mrs Stephenson as someone who cares, someone who is not just a bureaucrat. She spends time explaining the need to gather information, setting it in a wider context, where it is clear that this is not an end in itself. This is an important skill, which enables workers to maintain a sense of their professional identity and to establish a personal engagement with service users. (Skills for engaging with service users are covered more fully in the next chapter).

You may feel that this is over-optimistic. Certainly, there are occasions when the procedural framework may be more rigid and limiting than in this example. But in situations where workers are concerned about the negative impact of over-rigid procedures, they should be able to raise this matter in supervision, using the mediating function of supervision to send feedback to management. For more serious or widespread concerns about procedure, a more collective approach by workers may be needed; but the principle is the same. Workers should have an influence on shaping and developing procedures.

Skill summary: Using standardised procedures with sensitivity to individuals

Bringing the two together is difficult and requires a clear understanding of the statutory function of the agency and of its procedures, combined with good communication skills and an ability to deal empathically with individuals. Elements of this skill include:

- knowing the procedural requirements well, so as to be able to improvise around them
- explaining to service users the place and purpose of procedures
- being prepared to question aspects of procedure that don't seem to fit with professional values.

Learning this skill will help you to meet the following National Occupational Standards:

Key Role 1: Unit 2 and Unit 3.

Conclusion

The introduction to this book raised some fundamental questions about whether or not creative and anti-oppressive practice is possible in the current organisational context of statutory social work. This chapter does not attempt to minimise the difficulties. Nonetheless, it offers some pointers as to how social workers can develop the skills and confidence to work cooperatively with their managers in the interests of service users. How managers can acquire the corresponding skills is the topic for another book altogether. It should be clear that, despite the basic power imbalance which is inherent in the relationship between employer and employee, the best outcomes will only be obtained when this imbalance is not allowed to dominate the relationship and both parties respect the other's contribution. The same is true in relationships with service users, as we will see in the following chapters.

FURTHER READING

Hughes, L. and Pengelly, P. (1997) *Staff Supervision in a Turbulent Environment*. London: Jessica Kingsley Publishers. Explores how the dynamics of the supervisory relationship can be understood in relation to the environment in which it is taking place and argues that the 'thinking space' created in supervision is necessary for safe and effective practice.

Morrison, T. (2001) *Staff Supervision in Social Care: Making a Real Difference for Staff and Service Users*. Brighton: Pavilion Publishing. A detailed guide to the practice of supervision.

Tsui, M. (2005) *Social Work Supervision: Contexts and Concepts*. Thousand Oaks, CA: Sage. An exploration of the theoretical basis for social work supervision.

4

Skills for Engaging with People

Chapter summary

This chapter is about starting to work with people towards whom the employing agency has legal powers and duties. The word 'engaging' encompasses a wide range of skills that are needed to get the work going. This early phase in the work includes: coming to an initial view about a referral; first meetings with those involved; and the process of establishing with them a basis for social work. A distinctive feature of statutory contexts is that help may not have been requested, and may even be actively resisted. With this specific context in mind, the present chapter covers:

- establishing the mandate for the work
- respecting the rights of service users
- building partnerships
- communicating with children
- dealing with violence, threats of violence and intimidation.

Skills for Establishing the Mandate for the Work

In civil law a mandate is a contract that allows one person to carry out work or to deliver services on behalf of another. In statutory contexts, social workers have a legal mandate to carry out certain duties and to exercise certain powers on behalf of public bodies. In order to carry out those duties successfully, social workers must get to know the people they are working with. They have to form potentially intrusive interpersonal relationships with them in order to make detailed assessments, sometimes over relatively long periods of time. And, as we saw in Chapter 2, people who are on the receiving end of statutory interventions can and do actively resist. This means that, although the legal mandate for intervention may be clear enough, on its own it is rarely enough to ensure an effective intervention. Successful statutory work will require an element of discussion, and even negotiation, with those affected over what is being done, why, and on what basis. This is what is meant by establishing the mandate. It is not that the basis for the work is unclear in law; rather the question is one of converting this legal mandate into a working relationship with the people involved that will allow social workers to carry out their duties effectively.

Case example 4.1

Darren is 15 years old, lives in England, and has been made the subject of a referral order under the Youth Justice and Criminal Evidence Act 1999, following an assault on another young person. Social worker Janet has the task of preparing a report to the Youth Offender Panel recommending the kind of action that will reduce the risk of his reoffending. Darren lives in a hostel for homeless young people, having fallen out with both parents, who are separated from one another. Darren's mother is white and English, and his father is black and born in Nigeria. Both parents have new partners, with whom they have had children since their separation. Darren said that he wanted to return to live with his mother, but she is concerned about the impact of his angry and unpredictable behaviour on her younger children.

The panel meeting is the place where a contract is agreed with the young person to reduce the risk of reoffending. This model encourages the active participation of the young person and, where possible, of the parents and victims. In this case the concern seems to be about Darren's ability to control his anger. It seems quite possible that this anger is linked, at least in part, to feelings of rejection from both parents. This means that Janet, the social worker, will have to get to know Darren and his family if the contract is to make sense to him in his specific situation. What might be the most relevant parts of an anger management strategy? The effectiveness of the contract may well turn on engaging Darren's commitment to it, even though the legal position is that this contract is being imposed on him. (Note that the legal system in Scotland in relation to youth justice is very different from the one in England and Wales, and has always considered children's welfare as an integral part of the Children's Hearing system. Engaging with young people is a key to this approach).

This process of engagement requires communication and interpersonal skills at a high level. Of course, such skills are needed throughout all social work, not just in statutory contexts. A body of theory, research and practice wisdom already exists. The question for this book is whether such ideas are applicable in statutory contexts, with or without adaptation. So, before we can turn to this question, the next section summarises some of the literature about communication skills and the way they can help in the formation of working relationships with service users.

Communication skills in social work

A recent review of the teaching and learning of communication skills in social work education has found that counselling skills, mostly derived from humanistic and client-centred approaches, are often taught in the belief that they are generally useful in social work (Trevithick et al., 2004). Anyone who has undergone social work training is likely to have encountered the work of Carl Rogers (1961) and to be aware of his claim that the necessary and sufficient conditions for personal change are that the therapist should display skills of congruence, unconditional positive regard and empathy. But are these skills generally useful in social work? Trevithick and colleagues point to difficulties related to this assumption. In their view,

> there is little attempt to analyse critically the relevance of counselling theory to social work. As a result, insufficient attention is paid to the difficulties inherent when trying to apply concepts such as empathy to fieldwork settings, *particularly statutory social work* (Trevithick et al., 2004: 14, my italics).

Koprowska (2005), on the other hand, takes a much broader approach to communication and interpersonal skills in social work. She summarises the findings of three recent research studies into social work with foster carers, young people and older people respectively. In each case, the views of service users form a significant part of the study. Despite the wide variety of contexts, Koprowska identifies a number of interpersonal skills in social workers that lead to the formation of good working relationships. These skills are as follows:

- *Sharing of information* This could include providing information about confidentiality policies, complaints procedures, services available and any costs attached, the time available for discussion . . .

- *Developing a shared understanding of what the working relationship is about* This implies that purpose and goals are defined and negotiated. They can of course be reviewed and adjusted if they stop being a good fit. It also involves understanding people's perspectives and feelings.

- *Maximising choice and control* Most people want to feel in control of their lives and their decisions, and many service users have histories of being deprived of choice, by family, by professionals and by institutions . . .

- *Responsiveness* This can be fairly practical, like returning a phone call, or more emotional, in terms of sensitivity to the person's feelings in the moment, or remembering personal information in contexts when it may be aroused . . .

- *Reliability* This means doing what you said you'll do, when you said you'd do it – or having good reasons why you haven't been able to do so. Reliability significantly affects people's trust and confidence in you and in the service you represent . . .

- *Honesty* Honesty in terms of not stealing from or otherwise harming service users goes without saying. Here the meaning is more to do with people knowing where they stand. Can you secure them a place in a nursing home or not? What are the chances of their child being returned to them if they solve particular problems? Will you support them in opposing their detention under the Mental Health Act 1983 at this time? Can they see their father?

- *Unhurried pace* Several of the studies referred to the importance of feeling unhurried. Although real time makes a difference, pace changes the quality of whatever time you have available. Not only do people feel offended or that they don't matter if you are rushing them, they will usually communicate more clearly if they feel they have your attention and you are 'present'. So not rushing someone may actually mean you get to the point more quickly.

- *Respect* In a sense, everything else listed here refers by implication to a respectful approach. It is an overarching concept which relates to values, and the respect we accord to every person just by virtue of their presence in the world. (Koprowska, 2005: 31–33)

Differences in statutory contexts

We have already noted that there may be difficulties with the straight-forward application of Rogerian concepts such as empathy to statutory social work. Koprowska's list of skills has a similar flavour, being based on humanistic values that include a fundamental respect for the person. So what, exactly, are the difficulties, and to what extent are these interpersonal and communicational skills relevant to statutory contexts?

The central difficulty is that most of the literature on engagement assumes that service users are actively seeking help, even if they are anxious about change. So social workers should first engage service users through active listening and empathy and, once trust and coop-eration are building, they should move to problem assessment and intervention (De Jong and Berg, 2001). But, as Rooney (1992) and Ivanoff and colleagues (1994) have pointed out, where people do not want contact with social workers, empathy is unlikely to be enough to engage them. Instead, these authors argue that a social worker should seek to develop what they call 'motivational congru-ence'; in other words, that a social worker should seek to maximise the fit between what the service user wants and what the social worker is trying to achieve. Rooney and Ivanoff and colleagues are quite realistic in their approach to this idea. They argue for a twin-track strategy, of being very clear about elements of the inter-vention that reflect the statutory mandate and are non-negotiable, whilst at the same time maximising the person's sense of understand-ing, choice and control over all other elements of the intervention. This strategy reflects a commitment to anti-oppressive practice and to the principle of minimal intervention, and it also maximises the opportunities for empowerment and partnership. Nonetheless, it does not altogether solve the difficulties of anti-oppressively practis-ing in statutory contexts, which were noted in Chapter 2; and we will consider potential ways forward as we discuss each track of the strategy.

But first we should note the fit between this strategy and the skills listed by Koprowska (2005) and recorded above – skills for forming working relationships with service users. Significantly, the research studies that Koprowska draws on relate to social work in statutory contexts, namely fostering, social work with young people leaving care (a specific legal duty on local authorities) and the provision of local authority home care for older people. Several of the elements fit well with the twin-track strategy proposed by Rooney (1992) and by Ivanoff and colleagues (1994). Honest sharing of information reflects the first strategy, whilst maximising choice, control, responsiveness and reliability and adopting an unhurried pace reflect the second. We will now examine each track of the strategy in greater detail and consider possible ways of dealing with some of the difficulties.

Communicating concerns and responsibilities

In case example 4.1, one of the social worker's primary tasks is to explain to Darren the reasons for the initial visit, which should be in line with the principle of minimal intervention. Ivanoff and colleagues (1994) recommend that social workers should be clear, honest and direct. They also suggest that workers should openly acknowledge the involuntary nature of the encounter. This means clarifying:

- the role of the social worker
- what, if anything, the social worker is asking the service user to do
- how the social worker can be expected to respond to non-compliance
- what the service user may achieve through compliance
- the structure and format of this and any future contacts
- whom the social worker is reporting to, including any limits on confidentiality.

As a result of the first of these clarifications, Darren would receive information about the work of the youth offending team and, in general terms, about the extent of the team's responsibilities. Without this information, Darren would be at a disadvantage, so providing it can be seen as part of a strategy of empowerment. But the information in question needs to be given in a manner and at a pace that Darren can understand. It is known that people often find it more difficult to absorb this kind of verbal information when they are in stressful situations; hence it may be useful also to provide suitable explanatory leaflets.

But Darren will be anxious to hear what Janet is proposing to do in his case. It will be necessary to move on quite quickly to talking about the concerns raised by the offence and about the need to make recommendations to the panel about a suitable contract. Note that it would be natural to return to the topic of the agency's remit and responsibilities later, at the stage of discussing next steps.

Darren is also likely to be very concerned about possible negative outcomes, even if he doesn't say so. Will he end up in custody? It may not be possible to give a definite answer at this stage, but it is clear that the referral order, whilst designed to reduce reoffending, also has a welfare remit (Smith, 2007). The contract is likely to contain elements intended to help Darren to resolve some of the difficulties he has with his parents. Explanations of the social worker's role in relation to referral orders should mention not only the controlling element, but also the welfare element. As Trotter puts it: 'even when the focus of the work is on legalistic issues [. . .] it is important for the client to understand that the worker also has a helping role' (2006: 69).

Exercise 4.1

Imagine that you are the social worker who is preparing to visit Darren in case example 4.1.

a   Prepare a short leaflet explaining the role and responsibilities of the Youth Offending Team. Then practise giving this explanation verbally, preferably with someone else listening 'as Darren'.
b   Write down the explanation that you would give to Darren for this particular visit to him. Once again, practise this verbally, preferably with someone listening.

Skill summary: Communicating role and responsibilities

The first step in establishing the mandate for the work is to provide a clear explanation of the social worker's role and responsibilities. Not to do so is to disempower people. General information of this nature is best presented in written format, so that people may take it in later. But the information must also be given verbally, along with an explanation of the concerns arising in this particular situation. Good communication skills are important here. Skilled strategies include:

- being clear, honest and direct
- working at an unhurried pace
- showing respect for the person involved.

Learning this skill will help you to meet the following National Occupational Standards:

Key Role 1: Unit 1 and Unit 2.

Building working relationships

The second part of the twin-track strategy is also important. The objective is to maximise the person's sense of understanding, choice and control over elements of the intervention that are negotiable. In other words the goal is to maximise empowerment and partnership. Clearly, in statutory contexts the opportunities to build cooperative working partnerships vary greatly with the specific circumstances of the case. But, in general terms, those affected often have some interests that lead towards at least partial engagement. In our earlier example, it may well be that Darren was shocked and upset by his conviction, even if he doesn't show it. An element of mutual concern about his exclusion from the family home and about the reasons for it may provide a basis for some shared understanding and cooperation, despite the statutory context.

We have already noted that, even in statutory contexts, the social control element of the social work task is balanced by a helping role. But what skills on the part of the social worker might enable the development of working relationships that might be helpful?

Perhaps surprisingly, there is little research into the way in which social workers actually talk to service users in statutory contexts. There are ethical and practical difficulties inherent in researching these kinds of sensitive encounters. One recent attempt to find a way around the problem (Forrester et al., 2008) used actors who simulated parents, and it asked real social workers to interview them in typical child protection scenarios. The researchers found that, whilst almost all of the social workers were able to communicate clearly to the actor/parents the nature of their professional concerns about the children, many social workers showed low levels of empathy. Most importantly, the researchers noticed that the low levels of empathy led to increased resistance and a decrease in the amount of information offered. This fits with earlier research (Department of Health, 1995a), which identified child protection enquiries as confrontational and traumatic for parents. More positively, the few workers in the study by Forrester and colleagues (2008) who showed empathy created less resistance and were able to build positive relationships with the actor/parents.

So it seems that we have come back to the importance of empathy in building working partnerships. To summarise: it is clear that, in statutory contexts, empathy is unlikely to be enough, on its own, to facilitate engagement and to lead to partnerships. And in statutory contexts it is not usually possible or desirable to delay talking about the difficult topics until empathic communication has led to trust and cooperation. Encounters in statutory work are often more challenging than in counselling or therapy. Yet communicating concerns without empathy is likely to engender resistance and may lead to lost opportunities for cooperation and for the formation of helping relationships.

Skill summary: Building working partnerships

It should be acknowledged that the chances of building positive working partnerships in statutory contexts are strongly influenced by the particular circumstances of the intervention. In some situations such relationships may not be realistic. Nonetheless, good communication skills are always important. Research suggests that, although social workers may be good at communicating concerns, the frequent use of closed questions and the lack of empathy lead to considerable resistance and to the loss of opportunities for building working relationships. Strategies for skilled practice include:

- limiting the use of closed questioning
- recognising service users' strengths
- showing empathy for the position of service users
- looking for areas of common ground and mutual understanding
- maximising service users' choice and control over the negotiable elements of the intervention
- showing responsiveness, sensitivity and respect.

Learning this skill will help you to meet the following National Occupational Standards:

Key Role 1: Unit 1 and Unit 2.

Respecting Human Rights

In the previous section we have already seen the need for a respectful approach to service users. This is widely held to be one of the core values of social work; it is reflected in the British Association of Social Workers' Code of Ethics as follows:

3.1   Human Dignity and Worth
3.1.1   Value
Every human being has intrinsic value. All persons have a right to
well-being, to self-fulfilment and to as much control over their own
lives as is consistent with the rights of others.
3.1.2   Principles
Social workers have a duty to:

1   Respect basic human rights as expressed in the United
    Nations Universal Declaration of Human Rights and other
    international conventions derived from that Declaration;
2   Show respect for all persons, and respect service users' beliefs,
    values, culture, goals, needs, preferences, relationships and
    affiliations;
3   Safeguard and promote service users' dignity, individuality,
    rights, responsibilities and identity;
4   Foster individual well-being and autonomy, subject to due
    respect for the rights of others;
5   Respect service users' rights to make informed decisions, and
    ensure that service users and carers participate in decision-
    making processes;
6   Ensure the protection of service users, which may include
    setting appropriate limits and exercising authority, with the
    objective of safeguarding them and others. (BASW, 2002:
    2–3)

The idea of respect for the intrinsic worth of human beings is linked
to the related, but separate, concept of rights. But, whilst the 'Values'
statement in 3.1.1 implies an absolute respect for the intrinsic value
of human beings, it also states that an individual's right to control
over her or his own life may be limited by the rights of others. Later
on there is also a recognition that social workers may have to set
limits and exercise authority in order to safeguard service users and
others. In other words, respect for service users as people and respect
for service users' human rights are two different issues. Whilst both
are fundamental values in social work, nonetheless, in some circumstances in statutory work, the rights of individuals to freedom of
action may be limited by social work intervention in order to safeguard those individuals or others.

So what can it mean to respect someone as a person whilst at
the same time curtailing her freedom by exercising some legally
mandated authority? How can this fit with the principles of anti-
oppressive practice?

Case example 4.2

An approved social worker, Michael, has signed an application for a woman called Mary to be admitted to hospital in England for assessment under section 2 of the Mental Health Act 1983. (In Scotland, similar powers exist under the Mental Health (Care and Treatment) (Scotland) Act 2003.) Mary is 28 years old, white and British. She has been diagnosed by a psychiatrist as suffering from a mental illness, and she has recently taken a serious overdose of prescribed drugs. Now that she is in hospital, Mary is angry with Michael about her admission and she wants to know how she can 'get out of here' as fast as possible.

Michael is convinced that, in order for Mary to be kept safe for the time being, it is necessary that she remains in hospital for assessment. After all, this is why he signed the application in the first place. So why should he change sides, as it were, and advise Mary about her rights to appeal against her admission? Why should he help her to find an advocate or a lawyer to argue on her behalf, if he believes that to be discharged now would not be in her interests? Surely that would be a perverse thing for Michael to do. Perhaps it would be best for Mary if he were to do nothing.

In fact, such thinking is positively dangerous. These are precisely the kinds of situations where respect for the rights of people whose freedom is curtailed by statutory interventions is at its most important. Michael must understand that professional assessments cannot go unchallenged and that safeguards such as the right of appeal are very important. There are several reasons for this, including:

- the danger of professional misjudgement
- the danger of overuse of statutory powers where it is easy to exercise them
- the danger of workers becoming 'desensitised' to the seriousness of such interventions.

Michael is, quite rightly, accountable both to Mary and to the wider public for his professional assessment, as we saw in Chapter 1. It is clearly his duty to help Mary to exercise her right to challenge the hospital admission, paradoxical though that may seem. In fact this can be seen to be in line with anti-oppressive practice and with the principles of minimal intervention and empowerment. If Mary is empowered to the extent that she is able to use the appeals process, there is a greater chance that the intervention will be kept to a minimum.

There is some evidence emerging from research to suggest that, in practice, social workers are not good at empowering service users to challenge professional judgements, particularly their own. Social work agencies generally have policies that require social workers to provide service users with leaflets explaining how to complain and, where relevant, how to appeal. Yet compliance rates are often low (Banks, 2004), and systems for complaints and appeals may be generally lacking in rigour and independence (Amphlett, 1998). In research in Australia, McLaren (2007) found that social workers were reluctant to explain to parents that they, the social workers, have a duty to report concerns about children and therefore that there are real limits on the right to confidentiality. McLaren argues that the workers were trying to avoid the personal discomfort of giving such an unwelcome message. This appears to be a powerful dynamic in all such interactions. It is all too easy to avoid the discomfort that comes from a potential complaint or an appeal, particularly if you believe the complaint or appeal to be unwarranted, just by not providing the requisite information or support to the person who needs it. This procedure may also be used to conceal bad practice (Collingridge et al., 2001).

In fact, McLaren (2007) argues that being honest about the limited nature of confidentiality leads to better engagement. People appreciate a straightforward approach. Once again, this appears to be generally true; demonstrating respect for the rights of those affected by statutory interventions increases the possibility of engagement, even when people are opposed to those interventions. In some cases, but not all, a closer examination, by both sides, of the reasons for intervention may lead to a more highly agreed outcome.

Please note that this does not amount to an argument that social work should be allowed to police itself in this respect. Skilled practice that involves respecting the human rights of service users does not preclude the need for external scrutiny, for example by the ombudsman.

Skill summary: Respecting human rights

When the aim of a statutory intervention is to exert some control over an individual's behaviour in order to protect him or other people, it may seem perverse actively to uphold his right to challenge that intervention. Two very different arguments have been made for this. The first relates to the principles of minimal intervention and empowerment; the second, to maximising the opportunities for partnerships. Strategies for upholding service users' right to challenge interventions include:

- providing written information about complaints and appeals procedures
- providing information about the right of access to files
- being clear about the legal 'mandate' for the intervention
- where appropriate, explaining about advocacy services or rights to legal representation.

Learning this skill will help you to meet the following National Occupational Standards:

Key Role 3: Unit 10.

Building Partnerships

Statutory social work interventions can affect a wide range of people in different ways. There is a number of important distinctions to be made between the experiences, for example, of adults, children and young people, or between mothers and fathers, or between adults with learning difficulties and their carers. Each of these subjects can have differing attitudes towards statutory interventions and different working relationships with the social workers involved.

Case example 4.3

Amy is 12 years old. She lives with her mother, Carol, and Carol's partner of nine years, whose name is Ray. In the time they have been together, Carol and Ray have had two other children: John, aged 7, and Hannah, aged 5. The family is white, British and lives in England.

Recently Amy told her maternal grandmother, Pat, that Ray has been sexually abusing her whilst Carol was working nights. This had been going on for a long time. Pat was extremely angry; she confronted Carol and also phoned the police. When the police and a social worker arrived, Carol was in a state of shock. Amy was interviewed and had a medical examination and, later, Ray was arrested. He was subsequently charged and, a year later, convicted of several counts of rape and indecent assault. Amy gave evidence at the trial. During the year leading up to the trial, with skilled social work support, Carol gradually moved from initial shock, disbelief and some anger towards Amy to a position of believing and fully supporting her daughter and to separation from Ray. Ray's family lived locally and continued to believe his denial of the offences. After the trial, Amy's half brother, John, became very upset and angry with Carol and Amy and began committing petty offences in order, as he put it, to be able to go to prison with his dad.

Exercise 4.2

Consider three groups of people in case example 4.3 who have been affected by the statutory intervention:

- those to whom the local authority has a clear legal duty
- those living with them or caring for them
- wider family, friends and social networks.

Think about the likely impact of the intervention on specific individuals within the case study. Can you see any possibility of building a working partnership with any of them?

First there are those to whom the local authority had a clear legal duty.

- *Amy*   In this case, the local authority had a duty to Amy to make enquiries under s.47 of the Children Act 1989, to see whether any action was needed to safeguard and promote her welfare. Amy had told her grandmother because she wanted the abuse to stop, but she had been too scared to speak to her mother. Amy had been concerned about the impact of splitting the family up. So there was a clear opportunity to build a working partnership with Amy, with the shared goal of ending the abuse. But note that Amy was, with good reason, ambivalent about some of the likely professional strategies for achieving this, such as arresting and prosecuting Ray and preventing his return to the family. She did not want to cause that amount of distress to the others. So there were tensions in her relationship with her social worker, and these had to be addressed in order to engage with her.

- *John and Hannah*   The local authority has a duty under s.17 of the Children Act 1989 to promote and safeguard the welfare of the other children, John and Hannah, as children in need. Both these children felt the impact of their father's removal from home, and John was struggling to grasp the meaning of his father's being a sex offender. A working partnership with him might be built around his desire to understand and come to terms with what has happened, even though his desire to have his father back cuts across the aims of the professional intervention and, once again, creates tension in his relationship with his social worker. The needs of boys caught in such circumstances are complex and often overlooked (Hill, 2003).

The second category or group includes the parents and/or carers of those to whom the local authority has a legal duty.

- *Ray* Sometimes, as in this case example, one or more parent or carer may be suspected of abuse, and the intervention may be intended to control some aspect of their behaviour. In such cases there may not be any opportunity for a meaningful working partnership. In our example, Ray continued to deny the offence even after his conviction. Nonetheless, communicating concerns and respecting his rights continue to be relevant social work skills.

- *Carol* Here the position is altogether more complex. Feminist writers have pointed to the practice of unfairly blaming mothers, especially in cases of sexual abuse perpetrated by men (Hooper, 1992; Salter, 1988). The literature about child protection practice has tended to focus first on whether mothers had any knowledge of (and therefore, by implication at least, responsibility for) the abuse and, second, on assessing their ability to protect (for example Smith, 1995). This is beginning to change as a result of an increasing awareness of the impact on women of finding out about their children's being abused (Hooper, 1992) and as a result of the realisation that many, like Carol, change their position over time (Calder, 2001). In the initial crisis, a meaningful partnership with Carol in order to protect Amy looked unlikely, because she was stunned and not sure how to react. However, rather than label her permanently as an 'unprotective mother', Carol's social worker helped her to make a transition to understanding and believing Amy. This led to a genuine partnership between the two of them in protecting Amy and meeting the therapeutic needs of all three children.

The final category includes wider family, friends and social networks. Whilst social workers may have less direct contact with this group and there may, quite properly, be real limits on the amount of information that can be disclosed, nonetheless statutory interventions can have a wide impact and people in this category can become significant allies.

- *Pat*   In this case Pat, Amy's grandmother, was a key ally for Amy and for the social worker in the first few days of the intervention. The difficulty for the social worker was that Pat was forceful in her desire to see Ray punished, whereas both Amy and Carol were, in the early stages, ambivalent. This meant that forging too strong a partnership with Pat risked alienating Carol, in particular.

This is an example of some of the complexities of power relationships in families, which were referred to in Chapter 2. It points to the fact that the social worker's use of power is experienced differently by different people, and the polar opposites of being against or in favour of the intervention are not enough to describe the complexity of different family members' relationships to the social worker. Given the statutory duties, what constitutes a minimum intervention is different for each person. Partnerships take different forms, and the degree to, and context in which, the social worker might seek to empower different family members also varies widely.

Skill summary: Building partnerships

Although it may not be common for the objectives of individuals affected by a statutory intervention to coincide precisely with the aims of the social worker, nonetheless there may be enough common ground to allow for meaningful partnerships with some of these individuals. In addition, positions are not always fixed, and it may be possible to hold open the door for partnerships in the future. Skilled social work practice seeks to build partnerships with relevant individuals in order to further the aims of the work. Strategies include:

- a thoughtful analysis of the positions taken by all those affected
- the acknowledgement of areas of agreement and disagreement
- the avoidance of unnecessary disagreements and of backing people into corners

- highlighting and building on areas of agreement
- wherever possible, allowing time for change.

Learning this skill will help you to meet the following National Occupational Standards:

Key Role 1: Unit 1 and Unit 2.
Key Role 2: Unit 5 and Unit 9.
Key Role 4: Unit 12.

Communicating with Children

In case example 4.3 we considered in particular the perspectives of Amy and John. So how was that understanding gained? Communicating with children and understanding their wishes and feelings is an integral part of statutory work with children. Yet, to some people, getting down on the floor with the toy box and 'just playing' is not serious enough to fit with the legal duties of a professional social worker. How can we base our assessment of a child on a fundamentally frivolous activity such as play, when such serious decisions have to be taken? Perhaps play work should be left to specialist therapists who don't have to carry statutory responsibilities?

Being able to engage with children about difficult issues at stressful times in their lives is a difficult but essential skill for the statutory social worker to have. In many cases there will not be anyone else to do this work. The need to do it is embedded in the legislation itself. In England and Wales, Section 22 of the Children Act 1989 places a duty on the local authority, as far as its representatives can, to ascertain and give due consideration to the wishes and feelings of any child they are looking after or planning to look after. Section 53 of the Children Act 2004 extends the same requirement to the provision of services under s.17 of the Children Act 1989 and to child protection inquiries under s.47 of the Children Act 1989. Ascertaining children's wishes and feelings means entering their world and, for younger children at least, this includes communication through play. So social workers in the context of statutory child care need skills for a number of very different settings and very different ways of communicating. They need skills for playing in sand and water with young children, skills for working with young people, skills for presenting information and for making formal arguments in court, and the flexibility to make transitions between these very different ways of presenting themselves.

There is, of course, a large and helpful literature on the general topic of engaging and communicating with children (see the recommended reading at the end of this chapter). Here I shall summarise some of the main themes of this material very briefly, before moving on to consider, one by one, the relevance of each case to statutory contexts in particular. Note that it is not just social workers in children and families teams who need to have these skills. It is true that the skills in question are important in work with children and families, including work in the following areas:

- assessments to establish if children are in need, or at risk of significant harm
- work with children who are looked after by the local authority, including those leaving local authority care
- juvenile justice
- work with disabled children.

But a wide range of adults may care for children, and some of these adults may themselves require statutory services, for example in relation to mental health, problems of substance misuse, or older age. Social workers working with such adults also need to be able to communicate with their children and to be alert to the need for making links with other services if necessary.

Child development: Language and play

Knowledge about child development is important for communicating with children (Department of Health, 2002c). During their second year, children begin to acquire language rapidly, although the rate varies from child to child. Storytelling and the use of story books helps children to understand narrative, and they soon start to tell simple stories and to communicate verbally (Buckley, 2003; Jones, 2003).

Koprowska provides a helpful list of things to do and things to avoid when talking with children. Here are some of them:

Do:
- Encourage the child to tell you if you get in a muddle or get things wrong;
- Model this for them by saying when you don't understand;

- Encourage the child to tell you if they don't know the answer to something you ask;
- Slow down;
- Use short sentences;
- Use simple language;
- Give choices;
- Ask one question at a time [. . .].

Don't:

- Talk at length – make turns short or the child may lose the thread;
- Ask yes/no questions; younger children tend to answer the same way each time (no is more common in English);
- Ask leading questions;
- Use questions with a negative form: 'Do you not like school?'
- Ask why questions [. . .]. (Koprowska, 2005: 104–5).

Developing in parallel with language skills during the second year and onwards is the important phenomenon of imaginative play. Children begin to use objects so as to represent things or people; they act out stories in which people have imagined voices, wishes and feelings. It is suggested that playing out these stories helps children to learn to process and to regulate emotion, and that the process is linked to the development of lifelong 'self-talk' (Buckley, 2003).

It is necessary to be able to enter into a child's world of play, either as a means of relaxing children so as to make them able to discuss other, perhaps more difficult topics, or as a means of communication in itself. As a rule, children do not find it easy to sit and talk for long; hence social workers must be comfortable with a full repertoire of age-appropriate toys, games and creative activities. Sometimes you may be able to use a suitably equipped play room, perhaps in a local children's centre, but it will also be necessary to improvise play in other settings, such as the child's home. If you are using a car for visits, then it is a good idea to carry a play kit with you permanently. The following list of things you might include draws on Brandon and colleagues (1998), on Bannister and Huntingdon (2002) and on my own practice:

- soft toys
- small figures/animals
- hand puppets
- toy telephones
- cars, fire engine, ambulance

- paper, pens, crayons
- play-dough or fast drying clay
- small sand tray (with tight fitting lid!)
- collage materials and glue
- 'ice-breaking' board game.

One of the most challenging features of the most difficult kinds of statutory work is its powerful emotional content. There is evidence that children who are regularly in heightened emotional states find it harder to learn language and cognitive skills, and may therefore be less able to express themselves (Cross, 2004). Work may often focus on helping children to understand and to express difficult emotions, sometimes through the use of structured methods such as asking them to draw body maps or feelings faces (Department of Health et al., 1997). Note that, whilst there is a debate in the literature between those who advocate the use of such structured methods and those who advocate non-directive approaches (see, for example, Wilson et al., 1992), there is little evaluation to help with deciding the issue. Note also that this emotion also affects workers. It is quite usual to feel angry and sad about the harm that children suffer, and good supervision is essential if these feelings are to be managed effectively (see Chapter 3).

The power of adults

It is very important to be confident, relaxed and skilled at communicating with children verbally and through play. But even the most skilled workers continue to operate within a dynamic in which they have more power than the children they work with. In part this situation stems from just being an adult and having a certain amount of taken-for-granted authority over children. The power inherent in the social work role adds to the dynamic. So what effect does this have on our communication with children?

We must take steps to counter children's tendency to defer to us as adults and to tell us what they think we want to hear. This can be achieved partly by taking care to frame questions in a neutral manner – not in such a way as to suggest the answer. We can also counter the tendency by checking carefully that children do understand what we say to them; because there is a danger that they may appear to agree when in reality they do not understand. But children's responses are also shaped by the way they understand the social work role. Many will have little or nothing to work on in this area; and, in the absence of a reasonable explanation, children are very likely to invent their own, often with unforeseen consequences. One child whom I worked with eventually told me that he thought I must be a long-lost cousin of his dad's who, so the family story went, had stolen things from them before disappearing. This was, to his mind, why I had been allowed nowhere near his toys! But giving child-friendly explanations about social work is a surprisingly difficult thing to do. As with adults, having this information in a written format too is highly recommended.

The role of parents

There is a danger that the influence of parents on social workers' communications with children may be overlooked. For all children, arrangements to see them will be made usually with those carrying parental responsibility. In the case of younger children, these adults will also give their consent to the work. Few children have independent access to statutory social work services. This means that parents have an influence over the arrangements for social work contact with their children; they will often introduce the social worker and explain to the child about the role of social work.

Yet, in statutory contexts, it may be the behaviour of some of these adults that is the cause for concern. In the next chapter we will look at ways to negotiate with adults over arrangements for assessment in statutory work, including assessments that involve work with children. For now, the point is that parental attitudes towards the involvement of social workers are likely to have a significant bearing on how the child understands the social worker's role and on what they are prepared to say to him or her. This is a problem with no easy solution; one has to be constantly aware of the possible influences on children.

In addition, children may be influenced differently by different adults. In our earlier example 4.3, Amy was worried about repercussions from her step father if she was to tell about the abuse; worried that her mother might be angry; worried that her telling might split the family up – and yet she wanted the abuse to stop. Amy's relationship with her social worker cannot be fully understood without considering this complexity. Ascertaining children's wishes and feelings in such situations requires skill.

Skill summary: Communicating with children

The legal duty to ascertain children's wishes and feelings in a variety of different situations means that the ability to communicate with them is essential in statutory work. Workers may also encounter children in situations where the main statutory focus is on an adult carer; so the skill required for such communications must extend over a wide variety of settings. Strategies include:

- using child-friendly written and verbal explanations of the social worker's role
- using child-friendly verbal communication
- using play as a means of communication
- encouraging safe communication about difficult emotions
- understanding the influence of parents and others on children's communication.

Learning this skill will help you to meet the following National Occupational Standards:

Key Role 1: Unit 2.
Key Role 2: Unit 5.
Key Role 3: Unit 10.

Dealing with Violence, Threats and Intimidation

Even in statutory contexts, most encounters between social workers and service users do not involve any expression of overt hostility. Nonetheless, the National Task Force on Violence against Social Care Staff (2000) cites a survey indicating that a high proportion of the social care workforce has had some form of aggression directed at its members at some point in their career. In statutory contexts, where some of those affected by social work interventions may strongly disagree and make strenuous efforts to resist, the potential for aggression is higher than in other contexts for social work. And, although the possibility of aggression is there at any stage in the work, it is at the engagement stage, when the legal mandate for the work is first explained, that this potential is first activated. After all, it is easier to hurt someone with whom you have no connection. The present section of my chapter draws on the work of Braithwaite (2001) to look briefly at explanations for aggression, before it goes on to consider two elements of a safety strategy: anticipating aggressive behaviour and responding to it.

Aggressive behaviour can take a wide variety of forms. In addition to physical or sexual assaults, these can include shouting, swearing and making threats, verbally or in writing, with or without a weapon. They may also include the invasion of personal space; and they may not even be obvious. A colleague of mine was seriously threatened by a well-dressed man who gained entry to a shared office and sat on her desk, close up to her, speaking so quietly and gently that the rest of us assumed that he was a visiting colleague. The effective management of aggression is not only the responsibility of individual workers. There needs to be a workplace culture that does not tolerate aggression and where there is an effective staff safety policy.

Various explanations for aggression have been offered; here are some of them.

- Aggression is innate, perhaps an evolutionary trait.
- Aggression is learnt, either as a cultural norm or through rewards.
- Aggression is a consequence of earlier bad relationships.
- Aggression is caused by frustration.
- Aggression arises from competition for resources.
- Aggression is caused by altered brain chemistry (Koprowska, 2005: 142–3).

However, these explanations miss out the possibility that fear might account for aggression. This is often relevant in statutory work, where people may be frightened of the power social workers have, or the power they imagine that social workers have – for example that of removing children.

Predicting aggression

It seems that everyone writing about the prediction of aggression is agreed on one thing: that past violence is the best predictor of future violence, no matter whom it was aimed at (Braithwaite, 2001). But a careful consideration of the details of aggressive behaviour, if they are known – for instance from information about drugs or alcohol abuse – may help to prevent unwarranted fear, and also to put together a plan for dealing with this behaviour. Factors related to the context in which the encounter is taking place are also important. Braithwaite (2001) singles out situations in which people are threatened with the removal of children or the loss of liberty as being particularly dangerous, and argues that two workers are always necessary. As he observes, this has become common practice in child protection work, but it may also be needed during compulsory admissions to mental hospitals and care homes. It is also necessary to pay careful attention to the arrangement of practical issues such as where the exits are; whether there is any potential help; whether there are objects to be thrown; whether anyone else knows where I am – and so on.

Managing aggression

No matter how skilled we are, it is probably unrealistic to think that all aggression can be predicted and avoided. Once someone has started to behave aggressively, the options may be limited to trying to use verbal and non-verbal communication so as to manage difficult situations. Non-verbal strategies include:

- avoiding face-to-face confrontational stances by positioning yourself at an angle
- maintaining enough physical distance between yourself and the aggressor (two arms lengths when standing)
- not touching the aggressor
- not smiling – this is likely to invite 'What are you laughing at?'
- making enough eye contact without staring
- using gentle, free-flowing hand signals
- avoiding repetitive movements (Braithwaite, 2001: 77–84).

Verbal strategies include adopting an assertive and confident approach (Braithwaite, 2001; Butterworth, 2004; Mason and Chandley, 1999). Braithwaite recommends naming the person and their behaviour, describing the impact it is having on you and then requesting that they stop:

'Mr Jones, you're shouting. I find it offensive. Please, stop shouting and tell me about your mother's situation' (2001: 95).

However, as Braithwaite acknowledges, this method takes practice and it may not always work.

Skill summary: Dealing with violence, threats and intimidation

This is not just the responsibility of individual workers; it demands an agency-wide response. Dealing with violence is particularly relevant in statutory work in situations where people may feel threatened with the removal of their children or the loss of liberty. Safety strategies include:

- prediction: this is where the key issue (but not the only one) is a careful assessment of any previous incidents of violence and of the context of the current encounter
- management: this includes a range of non-verbal and verbal assertive communication skills.

Learning this skill will help you to meet the following National Occupational Standards:

Key Role 4: Unit 13.

Conclusion

In statutory contexts, the process of engagement is often difficult when those affected are resistant to a legally mandated social work intervention. The principles of anti-oppressive practice are highly relevant insofar as social workers seek to keep such interventions to a minimum level, to empower and cultivate partnerships with those with whom they are working. One way of achieving such aims is to provide clear information about any concerns; about the remit of statutory agencies; and about rights to appeal or complain. Showing empathy at the same time improves the chances of forming productive partnerships.

Yet we must maintain a critical stance towards the operation of these principles. For example, it would obviously be counter to the statutory duty to safeguard children if the social worker were to seek to work in partnership with a sex offender such as Ray and to do it on the latter's own terms, which could lead to continued abuse. But productive partnerships may be possible with other family members – and even, on the right terms, with Ray. We should think carefully about the possibilities for forming differing kinds of partnerships with a wide variety of people, who agree to various degrees with the aims of the statutory intervention, and not all of whom will be the subject of the legal duty. This is highly skilled work.

Further Reading

Braithwaite, R. (2001) *Managing Aggression*. London: Routledge. This book is specifically written for staff in social work and social care and is full of practical ideas.

Crawford, K. and Walker, J. (2003) *Social Work and Human Development*. Exeter: Learning Matters. Contains an introductory account of child development written for social workers.

Koprowska, J. (2005) *Communication and Interpersonal Skills in Social Work*. Exeter: Learning Matters. A clear guide to communication skills, with careful attention paid to the emotional content of communication in social work.

Luckock, B. and Lefevre, M. (eds) (2008) *Direct Work: Social Work with Children and Young People in Care*. London: BAAF. A collection of imaginative strategies.

NSPCC, Chailey Heritage, and Department of Health (1997) *Turning Points: A Resource Pack for Communicating with Children*. London: NSPCC. A treasure trove of practical resources for use with children.

5

Skills for Assessing and Planning

Chapter summary

This chapter considers the processes of assessment and planning in statutory contexts. It argues that skilled social workers maximise the opportunities for people to exercise choice and control over the assessment process, in line with the principle of empowerment. However, statutory contexts impose significant limits on the freedom of action of all those involved in assessment work. The chapter considers the skills for working creatively within these limits. It considers skills for ethical record keeping, for working with other professionals on assessment, and for making sense of the information that is gathered during a statutory assessment.

This chapter does not aim to give a comprehensive account of social work assessments. There are several excellent books on the topic, which are referred to in what follows and in the list of further reading at the end of the chapter. There is also additional literature on assessment with different groups of service users, for example in work with older or disabled people. Instead, this chapter stays with the central themes of this book. To what extent do the distinctive features of social work in statutory contexts require distinctive skills in assessment and planning?

First we should note that, although this discussion of assessment is separated from the discussion of interventions in Chapter 7, nonetheless the two are best thought of as aspects of a single, ongoing process. Carrying out an assessment is, in itself, a form of intervention and is very likely to lead to change of one sort or another. The very act of talking about a problem with a social worker can lead to changes in perception and in behaviour. The reverse is also true. Interventions often develop and move on from the original plan, in response to a changing assessment of the ongoing situation. The important thing is to understand assessment and intervention as being linked together in a single, cyclical process, which includes regular evaluation and review.

Second, we need to consider the concept of need. Many assessments in statutory contexts are defined as assessments of need. What are the needs of an individual older person under the NHS and Community Care Act 1990? Is this child 'in need' under the Children Act 1989? The difficulty here is that the concept of need is inextricably bound up with the process of rationing finite resources. So, in England, the government has issued eligibility criteria for access to services in adult social care, ranging from 'critical' through 'substantial' to 'moderate' and 'low' (Department of Health, 2002b). Similarly, the legal definition of 'children in need' can be seen as a way of ensuring that the duties of local authorities towards children do not amount to universal service provision. Like it or not, statutory social work assessments are, at least in part, about rationing resources.

Finally we need to consider three models of assessment that are often discussed in the literature. These relate closely to the discussion in Chapter 2 about the aims and purposes of social work and will form the starting point for our examination of assessment skills in statutory work. The following summary draws on Walker and Beckett's (2003) account.

- *The questioning model* This approach assumes that the social worker is the expert, can identify people's needs and should take responsibility for doing so. The worker has the power to ask the questions and controls the interpretation of what the service user says in response.

- *The exchange model* Here a common understanding of the problem and of what to do about it is arrived at through dialogue. This appears to be a more empowering model, where the service user may be an equal partner in the process.

- *The procedural model* This is a variation on the questioning model. The difference is that in this case the questions are defined in advance by the agency and they usually relate to eligibility criteria. They are often on pre-printed forms or require the entry of information into computer databases.

At first glance it seems obvious that the exchange model fits best with transformational views of social work such as we considered in Chapter 2. The questioning and procedural models, on the other hand, might be a better fit for statutory social work, insofar as it calls for the exercise of power by the social worker. However, in keeping with earlier arguments about the need to avoid unhelpful binary distinctions and about the potential for anti-oppressive practice in statutory contexts, the present chapter aims to show how a critical approach can lead to the appropriate incorporation of elements from all three models.

Setting Up Assessments

In the previous chapter we discussed meeting with people for the first time, clarifying the social work role and the mandate for the work, and beginning to build a working relationship. In most situations the next step will be to undertake some form of assessment. In some emergency situations there will be real urgency, and all this may be compressed into a very short time. But in this discussion we will assume that there is time to plan an assessment which will involve gathering and analysing information from several sources, and that its completion may take anything between one and a few weeks.

We will consider two very different case examples alongside one another, so as to illustrate some of the common skills that are needed in order to set up assessments in statutory contexts. Specifically, we will be examining the question of who controls the assessment. To what extent are these assessments shaped by government or agency procedures? How much discretion do social workers have over the process and content? What options are open to those who are being assessed? Is an anti-oppressive approach to assessments in statutory contexts possible and, if so, what would it look like?

Case example 5.1

Mrs Skinner is 76 years old and lives alone in a large house on the edge of an English town. Her neighbours contacted the social services department to complain about her. They said that she plays loud music at night and becomes verbally abusive if they complain. They were also concerned about her welfare. They said she is increasingly confused. A social worker has visited her and had a mixed reception. Mrs Skinner was initially hostile when the social worker explained the reason for the visit, but later she relaxed and seemed to enjoy the company. The social worker's initial impression was that the neighbours were right to be concerned. The house was cold and damp and in a bad state of repair. It seemed as though the gas cooker was no longer working and Mrs Skinner had been trying to cook over an electric bar fire. Mrs Skinner was born in Malta and, until recently, she had been getting help from a local Maltese community group. She said that she had told them to stop coming because they were always interfering.

Case example 5.2

For some time Mr Wheeler, a 40-year old disabled man, white and single, who lived in England, had been offered a comprehensive care package that included 'Meals on Wheels' and help with bathing and dressing. The problem was that he usually refused the care available. He had a long history of obsessive–compulsive disorder (OCD), in which his obsessive thinking and compulsions were about the need for cleanliness and for avoiding contamination. This was thought to furnish his reason for refusing care: he would not allow carers into his home for fear of contamination when they brought meals or touched the fixtures and fittings. He had several physical health problems that caused concern: type 2 diabetes, hypertension and vascular heart disease. Mr Wheeler was also partially sighted. Professionals involved in his care were concerned about a serious risk of fire, because he smoked heavily and, as part of the OCD, covered his tables and work surfaces with paper towels. Mr Wheeler lived in a block of flats.

At the moment Mr Wheeler is living in a residential home, having accepted this help when he was very frail. Now he wants to return home, despite the fact that his physical and mental health have not improved. Mr Wheeler's psychiatrist has suggested that he be placed on a Guardianship Order under s.7 of the Mental Health Act 1983. This would give:

- the power to require him to reside at a place specified by the authority or the person named as guardian
- the power to require him to attend, for example, a clinic or hospital, at places and times specified, for the purpose of medical treatment
- the power to require that any registered medical practitioner or Approved Mental Health Professional (AMHP) be given access to him.

Mr Wheeler has been referred to a social worker acting as an AMHP for assessment with a view to guardianship.

The statutory and procedural framework

Before we can consider the question of who is in control of these assessments, we must be clear about the statutory frameworks in which they are taking place. In the case of Mrs Skinner, the assessment will follow the Single Assessment Process (SAP) (Department of Health, 2002d). This is designed to standardise assessment in health and social care. The person who took the initial referral would have completed a SAP contact assessment. The social worker going to visit Mrs Skinner will be starting a SAP overview assessment. This might lead to a specialist assessment, for example in relation to mental health needs, through a General Practitioner (GP) referral to a psychiatrist or to a community psychiatric nurse. The expectation is that these assessments are shared with service users. Assessments for services are made in relation to the Fair Access to Care Services (FACS) criteria (Department of Health, 2002b). The local authority sets the point within the FACS structure at which they will provide services – for example, only for substantial and critical need but not for moderate and low need. Basic services which a social worker might consider for Mrs Skinner could be:

- a meal service of some sort
- support with shopping
- perhaps a home-care service for personal care.

However, the shopping service and other domestic support might be deemed moderate to low on the FACS criteria and might not be provided, unless the assessment indicates that these basic services are vital for Mrs Skinner's continued functioning. The outcome will be a care plan identifying Mrs Skinner's 'eligible needs' (again, a FACS concept) and ways in which these will be met.

In the case of Mr Wheeler, the assessment relates to the criteria contained in s.7 of the Mental Health Act 1983. The *Code of Practice: Mental Health Act 1983* (Department of Health, 2008) gives guidance on the individual professional responsibility of the AMHP. This includes ensuring that the patient is assessed 'in a suitable manner' and that the patient is ordinarily given the opportunity to speak to the AMHP alone.

The social worker also considered whether Mr Wheeler lacked capacity under the Mental Capacity Act 2005. However, Mr Wheeler was fully able to understand what guardianship meant. He was opposed to it and said that he would attempt to kill himself if he was forced to live in residential care permanently. The social worker had to weigh this against the risks associated with his return home. Note that, although Mr Wheeler's GP and his psychiatrist had recommended guardianship, nonetheless it is the role of the social worker, as AMHP, to consider the social circumstances, look for the least restrictive option and, where appropriate, to counter the medical opinion.

Professional roles

Exercise 5.1

Walker and Beckett (2003) identify a number of possible roles for social workers. These include:

- care management: setting up and coordinating services provided by others
- rationing: collecting information relating to criteria for the allocation of resources
- advocacy: speaking on behalf of other persons, or helping them to speak for themselves
- quasi-parental care: looking after children
- quasi-parental responsibility: exercising responsibility for children and for adults with limited decision-making capacity
- counselling and therapy: using the worker's relationship with the service user professionally, so as to promote change
- policing: regulating behaviour through the use of statutory powers.

Consider the two case examples 5.1 and 5.2. In the light of the legal and procedural framework that applies, which of the above social work roles might be relevant to each case?

In Mrs Skinner's case, the first two of these possible roles (care management and rationing) fit closely with the statutory and procedural frameworks. However, the statutory and procedural frameworks do not completely define the scope for social work assessment and intervention in either case. Other roles may be relevant, as follows:

- *Advocacy* There may be considerable scope for acting as an advocate for Mrs Skinner. One goal might be to understand Mrs Skinner's needs from her own point of view and then to work on her behalf, so as to make sure that her own assessment of her needs is met. But note that this goal is in tension with the ration-

ing role. Other possible advocacy roles exist, for example in relation to concerns about the physical state of the house. This may
be an area to include in the assessment, with a view to referral to
a local service for improving or repairing private homes. Grant
help might be available in the form of what is often called a
'Staying Put' grant. Similarly, concerns about Mrs Skinner's social
isolation might be addressed by trying to reintroduce the cultur-
ally appropriate Maltese community group, and there might be
room for an advocacy role in putting over her point of view, so
that the relationship works better in future. The social worker
may even end up acting as Mrs Skinner's advocate in the dispute
with the neighbours.

- *Counselling or therapy*   Workers often complain that they don't
  have time for this kind of social work. Some may consider it valuable, but old-fashioned. As we saw in Chapter 2, the main concerns of statutory social work seem to be maintenance and social
  control, not therapy. Nonetheless, Chapter 4 showed that communication skills derived from the world of counselling are essential in engaging with service users, and there is already some
  indication that Mrs Skinner values the contact with her social
  worker in its own right.

- *Taking quasi-parental responsibility*   Risk assessment would be
  vital and the local authority may have a separate risk assessment
  protocol for social workers to complete. In Mrs Skinner's case
  this would address the risks from cooking, but it would also look
  at the wider picture of confusion and social isolation. There are
  telecare options for monitoring physical risks (for example a
  smoke alarm connected to a telephone system; also natural gas
  detectors, falls detectors, 'wandering client' detectors, all linked
  to the same monitoring system). In addition, a mental health
  assessment might suggest the need to set up services to protect
  and support Mrs Skinner from potential self-neglect or harm to
  herself. She might be against such steps and, in circumstances of
  extreme risk, more formal steps under the Mental Health Act
  1983 could be considered.

- *Policing*   One of the neighbours' concerns was about noise. If
  they all lived in housing association accommodation, then this
  could be addressed by a housing officer. In private accommodation it is less clear what can be done, and certainly the social

worker would not carry any formal responsibility for policing Mrs Skinner's behaviour. Nonetheless, the noise in the night might relate to disorientation between night and day, so perhaps more daytime activities might be helpful. Perhaps Mrs Skinner could use a day-care centre or, more creatively, use Direct Payments to pay someone to take her out to do whatever she wanted to do.

In Mr Wheeler's case, the social worker's primary task was to determine whether or not quasi-parental responsibility should be taken for him, through statutory use of a Guardianship Order. In fact, the social worker concluded that such an order was not needed. As a consequence, several more of the above roles also became relevant in this case, as follows:

- *Advocacy* Having decided that an order was not needed, the social worker had a major role to play in speaking up for Mr Wheeler's interests in opposition to the views of his GP and psychiatrist. Given that they had both signed the appropriate recommendation forms, there was considerable pressure on the social worker to make the application.

- *Counselling or therapy* Getting to know Mr Wheeler may include elements of a therapeutic relationship if he begins to trust his social worker and to value his relationship with her. This may be particularly relevant when they are talking about Mr Wheeler's feelings about his situation and about his wishes for the future.

- *Care management* Although the referral for assessment under the Mental Health Act 1983 was restricted to questions relating to Mr Wheeler's mental health, nonetheless the key to Mr Wheeler's return home was to devise a care package that was acceptable to him and was sensitive to the difficulties caused by his OCD. The original assessment was broadened so as to include a community care assessment under the NHS and Community Care Act 1990, which in turn included other agencies.

Negotiating with service users about assessments

The preceding discussion gives a flavour of the complexities of the assessment task. In each case there is a clear legal and procedural framework, but within that framework there is a variety of possible social work roles. These roles imply different power relationships with service users. The policing role, for example, requires the explicit exercise of power over individuals, whilst the rationing role involves using power to determine fair access to resources, and the advocacy role implies a much more egalitarian relationship to service users. In order to decide which of these roles is needed, the assessment is likely to include discussion with the service user about each of them. A further complication is that some of these possible roles may be in conflict with one another.

It is time to return to the questions we started with. Who is in control of the assessment process? Is it the employing agency, through its assessment procedures; the social worker using professional skills; or the service user exercising some form of consumer choice?

Note that in neither case example did the service users ask for social work help. This is typical of statutory work, although, as we have seen, it is not a defining feature. Mrs Skinner was referred by neighbours and Mr Wheeler by his psychiatrist.

So: to what extent do these people have to cooperate with an assessment? What is in it for them? Are there parts of the assessment and of the potential social work roles that might be more acceptable to them than others? How much choice and control over the assessment do the people being assessed have in these statutory contexts? In other words, are there opportunities for empowerment and partnership to work?

Let us, again, consider the two case examples one by one. In Mrs Skinner's case the assessment for services was entirely voluntary. Whilst the referral suggested that she may be confused at times, nonetheless her mental state appears to be a very long way from the kind of threshold which might trigger an assessment under the Mental Health Act 1983. So Mrs Skinner is free to refuse an assessment and, indeed, her reaction to the first social work visit was initially hostile. This means that there would have to be a good deal of trust and relationship building in order for Mrs Skinner to accept the possibility of help and, therefore, the need for an assessment. These are the engagement skills that we considered in Chapter 4.

This process of reaching a shared understanding of the desirability of an assessment for services implies that the assessment itself could follow the exchange model, with Mrs Skinner as an equal partner in developing a shared understanding of her own needs. Yet in practice there are forms to fill in, and rationing of services to be done, and the procedural model of assessment could easily take over. One pragmatic response to these competing approaches is to work from the service user to the forms, rather than from the forms to the service user. In other words, instead of asking Mrs Skinner the list of questions on the form in the predetermined order and recording her responses, it may be possible to start with a conversation with her, as in the exchange model, and to complete relevant sections of the form as they arise in the conversation, or afterwards. This method would allow Mrs Skinner much more control over the process and would give a better indication of how she prioritises the issues. It requires the social worker to have a good working knowledge of the contents of the form, so as to recognise relevant issues as they come up. Towards the end, the conversation is likely to lead to a situation in which the social worker is aware that there are still questions scattered across the form which have been neither asked nor answered. Some of these questions may seem highly relevant, and the worker may be happy to raise them. Others may seem irrelevant, and here much will depend on the degree of flexibility built into the procedures. Certainly there are ethical problems with asking for information that does not seem to be relevant.

In Mrs Skinner's case, it might be helpful to obtain more information from the neighbours, from family if it is identifiable, and perhaps from the Maltese community group. However, all this should be within Mrs Skinner's control and should be done with her agreement.

In the second case example, the social worker will need to talk to Mr Wheeler himself. The statutory context sets the parameters of the assessment: the need to ascertain Mr Wheeler's wishes and feelings, the need to make some assessment of his mental capacity and of the various risks associated with each of the possible courses of action. However, there is still considerable scope for deciding how to go about obtaining the information needed for the report. As in the first case example, the order in which topics are discussed may be varied, so as to help with the process of building relationships. Detailed discussion of the most difficult topics may be left until later on in the process. In other words there is room for some negotiation about the topics covered and about the order in which they are tackled. Elements of the exchange model of assessment sit alongside the questioning and the procedural.

Skill summary: Negotiating over the content and method of assessments

In statutory work, the overall parameters of assessments are defined by the legal and procedural context and often there is detailed guidance, even about specific questions to ask. Nonetheless, there may be some space for varying the content and method of assessment, if only in small ways. Skilled workers will utilise this space in order to empower people, albeit in limited ways, and to build working partnerships and work around resistance. Strategies include:

- allowing people time to make their case
- varying the order of topics to be covered in assessment
- being clear about any elements of the assessment that are non-negotiable.

Learning this skill will help you to meet the following National Occupational Standards:

Key Role 1: Unit 3.
Key Role 3: Unit 10.
Key Role 4: Unit 12.

Recording Information

Record keeping is an important aspect of social work in statutory contexts. One of its main purposes is to ensure accountability to service users and, in some circumstances, to wider society, by documenting the basis on which assessment decisions have been made. This implies not only the recording of factual information, but also the recording of professional thinking and of the resulting professional judgements. However, it is widely accepted that good practice is to separate, as far as is possible, fact from opinion (Coulshed and Orme, 2006).

As with so many social work activities, there are additional, competing aims that add to the complexity of the recording task. Electronic records are being used increasingly for administrative purposes, including for quality control and budgeting, reports from databases being sent to central government. These records are likely to involve the completion of forms with predetermined items of fairly succinct information. Yet records are also vital in individual supervision, for the professional purposes of reflection and decision-making.

These are likely to include more detailed, perhaps reflective writing. And there has been a strong movement in favour of shared recording, in which service users play an active role in the preparation of records.

So what are the hallmarks of good recording practice in assessments in statutory contexts? The following draws on the work of Healy and Mulholland (2007) and Reamer (2005).

Timely recording

It is difficult to find a social worker who enjoys record keeping. Most seem to regard it at best as a necessary evil and, at worst, as a distraction from the 'real' face-to-face work. The temptation is to put it off until later. Yet delays in recording information can have serious consequences. They undermine the credibility of social workers' claims, because it is widely accepted that information recorded contemporaneously with the event is more likely to be accurate. Notes that were not made contemporaneously are unlikely to be admissible as evidence in court. Ideally, recording should take place either during the session with the service user or straight afterwards, but certainly within twenty-four hours.

An appropriate balance between detail and brevity

Knowing what to write down and what to leave out is difficult. Much depends on the context of the assessment and on the purpose of the recording, and it is important to distinguish between factual information and professional judgement.

With factual information, how much to record is largely a pragmatic judgement. The principle is to record the minimum necessary, as succinctly as possible, in line with the principle of minimum intervention. But deciding on a minimum level can be difficult and will vary in different contexts. In serious cases, assessment interviews can last several hours, and it may be appropriate to tape record the whole conversation and to transcribe it verbatim. Where service users have low levels of trust in professionals, this can give reassurance that what they said during the session will not be misrepresented, as well as providing professionals with a detailed and accurate factual record. On the other hand, in most situations verbatim recording would result in far too much detail. Yet it is obvious that there is an opposite danger, that of recording too little. Public enquiries into child deaths during the 1970s and 1980s regularly criticised the lack of record keeping in these cases (Munro, 1998). A similar finding in a more recent child care case, Re E (Care Proceedings: Social Work Practice) [2000] 2 FCR 297, led to the requirement that an up-to-date chronology should be kept at the front of each case file.

When it comes to knowing when to record professional judgements, things are more complex. It is important to realise that professional judgements must always be supported by evidence and that such evidence should be cited in the record. So, referring to case example 5.1, to write 'Mrs Skinner appeared confused' is not acceptable unless there is also a record of exactly what was observed that led to that conclusion. Similarly, hypotheses or suspicions about service users should not be recorded without supporting evidence. But here it is important to consider the weight of the evidence and how strong any suspicions are. Recording serious concerns about Mrs Skinner's mental health on the basis of flimsy evidence would be bad practice and, taken to extreme, might even constitute slander. It would be better to wait and see if substantial evidence emerges, for example evidence from doctors and, if so, only then to record such a view, together with the evidence for it.

Understanding the audience(s)

The problem here is that social work recording usually has more than one audience. It may be read by the subjects of the recording and by other professionals in a variety of contexts. It needs to be legible and to use proper grammar at all times. It must use clear, precise and unambiguous language, which avoids professional jargon and obscure abbreviations.

Acknowledging errors

Sometimes factual information that was recorded contemporaneously turns out to be incorrect. Sometimes we mishear, or we just make a mistake. And, of course, opinions probably should change as the evidence available is updated. Attempts to cover up errors or changes of opinion by going back and amending the record are not acceptable. If changes are made in anticipation of court proceedings or of enquiries of any kind, they may lead to allegations of contempt of court, or even of obstruction of justice. The proper response is to make a new entry, recording when and how the error was discovered, or why your opinion changed.

Skill summary: Recording information

Good recording is essential in statutory social work, yet the skills involved are often overlooked. Key elements are:

- completing the recording in timely fashion
- distinguishing between fact and opinion
- keeping as succinct a record as fits the purpose
- recording the evidence to support opinions
- using clear, precise and unambiguous language
- openly correcting any errors
- upholding service users' rights to see their personal records.

Learning this skill will help you to meet the following National Occupational Standards:

Key Role 5: Unit 16.

Making Sense of Information: Using Formal Assessment Tools

Assessment involves not only the gathering and recording of detailed information, but also its analysis. Social workers tend to be good communicators, and they seem to find it easy to acquire large amounts of information about people. But it can be more difficult to make sense of that mass of information, particularly when one is called on to make what are often stark, binary recommendations or decisions (for example as to whether to seek a Guardianship Order or not).

In many statutory contexts there are formal assessment tools, frameworks or protocols that are designed to help with the analysis, including the assessment of risk. This section considers the skills that are needed to use these tools effectively. By way of illustration we will consider the use of the *Framework for the Assessment of Children in Need and their Families* (FFA) (Department of Health, 2000b), presented in case example 5.3.

Case example 5.3

Martin has just been appointed as Children's Guardian for Mandy Wright, aged 6. Mandy is the subject of a care order following care proceedings in England. She has spent the last three years living with local authority foster carers. Mandy's mother, Toni, was a heroin user when the care order was made; but in the meantime she has separated from Mandy's father, who was also a heroin user, and she is now in a lesbian relationship with a new partner, Susan. Toni has applied to the court for the discharge of the care order, so that Mandy can come and live with her and Susan. She claims to have stopped using drugs. The local authority currently opposes this application, saying that it is too early to tell whether this apparently more stable lifestyle will last. Local authority social workers are concerned about the likelihood of continuing significant harm. As Children's Guardian, Martin must make an independent assessment of the situation and make recommendations to the court.

Research has suggested that the introduction of the FFA has 'improved the quality of assessments' (Cleaver and Walker, 2004: 250). However, it would seem that the reported improvement relates more to the systematic collection of information and to the improved record keeping than to its analysis. So what are the skills needed?

Summarising and weighting different assessment topics

The FFA provides a system for cataloguing information into three domains, each one with several critical dimensions, as shown in Table 5.1.

Table 5.1 Summarising Different Assessment Topics

	Domains		
	Child's developmental needs	Parenting capacity	Family and environmental factors
Dimensions	Health	Basic care	Family history and functioning
	Education	Ensuring safety	Wider family
	Emotional and behavioural development	Emotional warmth	Housing
	Identity	Stimulation	Employment
	Family and social relationships	Guidance and boundaries	Income
	Social presentation	Stability	Family's social integration
	Self care skills		Community resources

SOURCE Department of Health (2000) *Framework for the Assessment of Children in Need and Their Families*. London: The Stationery Office.

Seden (2001) provides a helpful account of the origins of this structure. The FFA encourages social workers to summarise the information gathered in each critical dimension. These summaries are then drawn together and further abbreviated to give the main findings in each of the three domains, which leads in turn to overall findings.

However, simply organising the information under these headings does little to help with decision-making. How do we know which information is the most important? Does the weighting given to each critical dimension vary from case to case? For example, in relation to Mandy it might be that the summary of information in relation to parenting capacity is positive, and yet Mandy is happy in foster care and wary of going home. Which is the most important factor: Mandy's concerns about going home, or the expectation of satisfactory care if she does so? In order to operate the FFA, social workers must necessarily find ways of evaluating the information in each critical dimension and of weighing them against one another. As Calder (2003) argues, such methods are not inherent in the FFA itself.

Analytical skills

One of the central problems with assessments is that, if we are not careful, they have a tendency to come up with the answer we first thought of. We tend to find evidence to back our first understanding of the situation. Parton (1998) suggests that dominant explanations are often formed at the referral stage and that they may be hard to shift. He also argues that we should not be shy of acknowledging that our conclusions come with a degree of uncertainty attached to them, and that there is no such thing as a correct interpretation of the information.

It has been suggested that the analysis of assessment information has much in common with the analysis of data in qualitative research (Holland, 2004). Here there are two common approaches to analysis. Inductive methods start by reading the data with a view to developing explanations that will hold true for as many of the observations as possible. On the other hand, deductive methods start with hypotheses or explanations and interpret the data in the light of these. In practice it may be desirable to combine elements of the two approaches. In social work assessments it will be necessary to test pre-existing ideas, for example that Toni and Susan may not yet be able to meet Mandy's needs. But it is also necessary to be open-minded about new understandings that may arise in the course of the assessment.

At the heart of this approach lies the need to challenge our thinking by systematically considering all the possible explanations or interpretations of the information. This moves us towards the notion of reflective practice: the idea that we should be critically aware of the impact on assessments of our belief systems and, indeed, of our own individuality. In the context of social research, McCracken (1988) suggests that we should carry out a 'cultural review' of our own assumptions about the topic before commencing the research. Shaw (1996) suggests that this may also be useful in social work practice. For example, the case of Mandy involved the assessment of the parenting capacity of a lesbian couple. So before we start we might ask ourselves:

- What do I know about parenting and lesbian couples?
- Where does this knowledge come from?
- What prejudices do I hold?
- What might I find surprising about this situation, and why?
- How will I be perceived by this couple?
- How will the assessment be understood by them?

The idea is to use our existing knowledge, but to create the space for that knowledge to be challenged. By bringing the couple's sexuality into the foreground we have opened up questions of structural oppression and of how it relates to parenting (Tasker and Bigner, 2007). The result will be assessments in which judgements are not merely stated, but where the value, theory and research base are made explicit and where recommendations are argued in relation to possible alternatives. We will return to the theme of report writing in the next chapter.

Assessing risk

The term 'risk' is used in lots of different ways in social work. For the sake of clarity it is important always to specify risk of what and to whom. Sometimes the concern is about risk of harm to a service user or about the risk of a service user harming other people. Sometimes the concern is about risk of harm to a professional, and sometimes it is about risk to the agency of damage to its reputation, or even of being sued if things go wrong. The last two possibilities have been considered in Chapters 3 and 4. In this section we are concerned with assessing any risk of harm to or from service users.

There are two different approaches to these kinds of risks in statutory contexts. On the one hand there are approaches that treat risk as a separate issue in its own right. Typically social workers may be asked to complete a risk assessment to a required format, which is separate from other elements of the assessment. One example is the ASSET assessment (Youth Justice Board, 2006). This is specified by the National Standards for Youth Justice in England and Wales and aims to assess risks that young persons might present to themselves, or to others, as well as risk of reoffending. In common with other such tools, the ASSET encourages workers to look for known risk factors in a young person's background, lifestyle and attitudes. Such approaches may require workers to assign numerical scores.

On the other hand, there are approaches that maintain a much broader focus. These may be known as comprehensive or holistic assessments, and risk is just one aspect of them. The FFA is an example. Such approaches seek to balance risk factors with protective factors and to give an overall picture.

At the extremes, there are dangers with both. Reviews of risk factor research suggest that these are at an early stage of development and should be used with caution (Corby, 1996). In the area of child welfare it has been argued that an over-emphasis on risk has led to a deficit in the attention paid to supportive services for families (Department of Health, 1995a). But, on the other hand, holistic assessments such as the FFA have been criticised for hiding the significance of risk (Calder, 2003).

What is needed is a balanced approach that draws on what is known about relevant risk factors and applies that knowledge to the context of an individual's overall situation. Whether risk is assessed separately or as part of a holistic assessment, skilled analysis of the information is still required.

Skill summary: Analysing information from assessments, including risk

Specific assessment formats or frameworks exist in many areas of statutory social work. These can be a useful aide-memoir, helping to ensure that relevant information is sought, and a useful conceptual tool for organising that information. However, they may be less helpful when it comes to making sense of the material, and it is here that an additional skill is required. Strategies for skilled analysis include:

- testing our pre-existing ideas about the situation, whilst at the same time remaining open to new ones
- challenging our own assumptions about the cultural issues raised in the assessment
- being aware of and explicit about the basis for our assessment – both the values we hold and the ideas from theory and research that have influenced us
- always considering the possible risks, and being clear about risks of what and to whom
- being prepared to consider alternative viewpoints, including the possibility of error
- where necessary, moving beyond any limitations of organisational frameworks for completing assessments.

Learning this skill will help you to meet the following National Occupational Standards:

Key Role 2: Unit 6.
Key Role 3: Unit 11.
Key Role 4: Unit 12.

Working with Other Professionals

Inter-agency and multidisciplinary working is a key element of assessment in many statutory contexts. It has obvious benefits where, as in the provision of community care, contributions from doctors, nurses, home carers, therapists and others are likely to be needed. It can prevent the duplication involved in multiple assessments and should lead to better coordination. Contributions from the specialist knowledge bases of a range of disciplines may be relevant to many assessments. In complex cases they can expose social workers to the kind of challenge to their thinking that may help with critical analysis.

This section considers the skills that are needed for successful assessment work with other professionals. However, it has long been noted that there are some significant barriers to collaborative working across disciplines, particularly in the context of child protection (Stephenson, 1989). These barriers may exist not only at the level of individual workers but also at the organisational level. Professional groups have different histories, cultures and status. The skills considered here may help, at least in part, in overcoming these barriers. However, as will become clear, it is not suggested that acquiring these skills at an individual level will provide a complete solution. Organisational and policy responses are also required.

Role clarity

Let us return to case example 5.1 concerning Mrs Skinner. If the social worker's first visit suggests concerns about her health, then her GP (or district nurse, if involved) might be contacted for information. Similarly, continuing concerns about Mrs Skinner's mental health might lead, through her GP, to a specialist assessment by a psychiatrist or by a community psychiatric nurse. Information from each of these sources would be brought together.

For this to happen, it is necessary for the professionals involved to have an accurate understanding of each other's statutory roles and responsibilities, and also of the professional values of each of the disciplines. So the social worker should be aware of any local protocols for information-sharing that might influence the GP's ability to disclose information about Mrs Skinner to the social services without her consent. In this case, disclosure is unlikely. Understanding this would almost certainly prompt the social worker in the first place to seek Mrs Skinner's agreement to approach her GP. Inappropriate expectations of other agencies cause irritation at best, and can become a barrier to collaborative working.

So how do professionals acquire this kind of knowledge about other disciplines? There is some limited research evidence to indicate that the introduction of assessment frameworks that are shared across disciplines leads to increased clarity about the roles and responsibilities of agencies, particularly when there is joint training (Cleaver and Walker, 2004). There is also an argument for professionals to have more contact with one another during qualifying training.

However, it should be acknowledged that the differing roles and responsibilities of agencies sometimes cause tensions that do not stem from a lack of clarity. For example, Davies (2008) laments what she sees as the recent minimisation of the role of police in child protection work: a withdrawal from joint investigations unless there is a clear primary focus on an allegation of a crime. More generally, shortfalls in resources may lead agencies to draw back from service provision, particularly where the service in question may be provided by another agency.

Open communication between agencies

Concerns about gaps in communication between agencies may be widespread in social work, but they have received particular attention in relation to child care. Time and time again, investigations into child deaths and serious injuries have been critical of the lack of communication between professionals (Reder et al., 1993). Whilst we should be wary of drawing conclusions about the whole of child-care work from the analysis of these very special cases, nonetheless concern about failure to communicate about the outcome of referrals and assessments has led to the introduction in England and Wales of a specific requirement to do so (HM Government, 2006: 107–8). Information sharing between agencies is set to take another step forwards with the implementation of s.12 of the Children Act 2004 and the establishment of ContactPoint, a common database of information about all children in England. The aim of official policy has been to increase the amount of information gathered and shared between agencies so as to coordinate services better.

Yet the process of information gathering and sharing is not without cost. Leaving aside recent concerns about the security of large electronic databases and the implications for civil liberties (Penna, 2005), 'the more time is spent on information gathering and information sharing, the less time is spent on anything else' (Beckett, 2007: 203). Beckett's argument is that, whilst it is necessary to gather relevant information, in the end there is a trade-off between information gathering and acting. Just as information collection during assessments needs to be targeted and relevant to the issues under consideration, so information sharing between agencies needs to be targeted and to have a clear purpose. We should resist the assumption that all the information we hold about service users should be available to all other agencies all the time. Even if advances in information and communications technology ever made this possible and if service users agreed to it, imagine the waste of time spent sifting for relevant material. Being skilled in inter-agency assessment work means using our insight into other professional roles in order to recognise information that may be relevant to other agencies and, taking account of data protection rules, sharing it appropriately.

**Skill summary: Working with other professionals
on assessments**

Inter-agency and multidisciplinary working is the norm in most statutory contexts. Other professionals are likely to be involved in assessments to a greater or lesser extent. Social workers need to be skilled in
working alongside them. Strategies include:

- having a clear understanding of the roles and responsibilities of the
  various agencies, including your own
- being able to identify information that should and can be shared
  with other agencies.

Learning this skill will help you to meet the following National Occupational Standards:

Key Role 5: Unit 17.

Conclusion

Assessment processes in statutory contexts are often tightly defined
by the nature of the legal duty and by the detailed agency procedures
that describe how these processes should be carried out. Such detailed
assessment frameworks reflect in part a strategy by employing agencies to ensure a standardised, high-quality response. They are a
response to the increasing pressure for accountability. As we saw in
Chapter 1, there is an argument that following detailed procedures
is deskilling for social workers. In this chapter we have seen how,
even within quite rigid statutory assessment frameworks, a skilled
and flexible use of the exchange, questioning and procedural models
of assessment can create opportunities for those being assessed to
exercise some choice and control over the process. Such a skilled
approach will also include recording practice that pays attention to
the rights of those being assessed. It will include analysis that is reflective and holistic and incorporates a structural understanding of
oppression and discrimination and an analysis of risk.

FURTHER READING

Healy, K. and Mulholland, J. (2007) *Writing Skills for Social Workers.*
London: Sage. Contains useful sections on writing case notes and a discus-

sion of ethical issues, including client confidentiality, privacy and empowerment.

Holland, S. (2004) *Child and Family Assessment in Child Care Practice.* London: Sage. The second part of the book is about the relationships between the various parties to assessments in child care and how they are negotiated.

Reamer, F. (2005) 'Documentation in social work: Evolving ethical and risk-management standards', *Social Work,* 50 (4): 325–34. An American article that helpfully links recording practice to the concept of risk management.

Walker, S. and Beckett, C. (2003) *Social Work Assessment and Intervention.* Lyme Regis: Russell House Publishing. An excellent introduction to models of assessment and the dilemmas of their use in a wide range of practice settings.

6

Skills for Court Work

Chapter summary

This chapter considers the skills for working with legal advisers in managing and preparing cases that go to court. It looks at the skills needed to prepare good quality written reports and statements for court, and at skills for giving oral evidence. Negotiations with other parties to the proceedings are an integral part of the process of going to court, and this chapter considers the skills that are needed to be successful. Finally it looks at the implications of continuing to work with service users during and after the court proceedings and at skills for managing working relationships in this difficult context.

Even in statutory contexts, most cases do not go to court. But the most serious and intractable cases may do so, and so must the social worker. This chapter is about the specific set of skills that are required for social work in the courts, or at quasi-judicial hearings such as mental health tribunals. Situations in which social workers may be required to attend court include:

- situations where the local authority has applied for a court order and the relevant social worker must attend on behalf of the local authority, for example when starting care proceedings
- situations where the local authority is responding to a case initiated by someone else, for example when a parent applies for the discharge of a care order and the social worker must attend on behalf of the local authority as respondent

- situations where the social worker is required to give evidence as a witness, either because he or she has factual information to give to the court or because the court is seeking the social worker's opinion as an expert. This can happen whether or not the local authority is a party to the proceedings.

The case example and most of the discussion in this chapter relate to the first situation, that of an application for a care order, but the skills involved have a wide application in court work.

Most people feel apprehensive when approaching court for the first time. In addition, some social workers may feel that the values of social work do not fit well with involvement in court proceedings. Anti-oppressive practice stresses the value of partnerships with service users, so that the confrontational aspects of court proceedings can be very uncomfortable for social workers and may even feel like a failure. Stereotypically at least, social workers do not like formality and they may be suspicious of the artificiality and theatricality of some proceedings.

But if we accept the need to go to court in the most serious cases, then it follows that social workers should accept the need to develop effective skills for court work. As Lynn Davis puts it:

> As a social worker, you are a member of a profession which constantly struggles to establish its credibility. There is still a perception that social workers lack skill and professionalism, sometimes leading to an independent expert being instructed in proceedings to do little more than validate the social worker's assessment. You owe it to yourself and your profession to challenge that perception by the quality of your work and your presentation. Only by consistently demonstrating that the courts can trust them will social workers achieve the respect they deserve. (Davis, 2007: 15–16)

Despite initial apprehension, some social workers become highly skilled in court work and take great satisfaction from doing this important part of their job well.

Working with Legal Advice

Most agencies involved in statutory social work have access to legal advice. Local authorities often have in-house lawyers, or sometimes they may use specialist lawyers in private practice. (The term 'lawyer' is used to include both solicitors and barristers). The lawyer's duty is to present the local authority's case in the most effective way. This means that the lawyer must:

- maintain the integrity of the local authority before the court
- examine the local authority's case at an early stage
- attend case conferences and formal planning meetings wherever possible
- obtain all necessary statements and ensure that all relevant information is before the court and other parties
- ensure that the statements accurately represent the witnesses' evidence and that the witnesses understand what is written in their statement and sign it
- meet strict timetable requirements. (Cooper, 2006: 17)

For social workers going to court, their relationship with their legal adviser is crucial. In this section we will examine this relationship. First we will consider some of the potential difficulties; then we will see how, in relation to a specific case example, these may be resolved.

There is some evidence that the relationships between lawyers and social workers can be difficult (Beckett et al., 2007; Dickens, 2006). These difficulties seem to revolve around different understandings of the working relationship between the two, and around different understandings of how to conduct cases.

In fact, the relationship between social workers and their lawyers in care proceedings may not be straightforward. In other situations the client might expect to give instructions to the lawyer, to receive advice and to decide what to do in the light of that advice. But when the local authority is considering an application to court, it may not be entirely clear who the client is. Strictly speaking, it is the local authority as a public body, but who speaks on its behalf? Is it the social worker assigned to the case; the social worker's manager; the chief executive; or the chair of the relevant committee? And if the lawyer is also employed by the local authority and has a responsibility to look after the local authorities' interests, then perhaps the lawyer should refuse to follow instructions from social work professionals that might involve a risk to the local authority?

Dickens' (2005) research shows that social workers tend to believe that lawyers should argue the case in accordance with social workers' instructions and should not question social work decisions, whereas lawyers are concerned to ensure that cases are based on strong evidence and clear analysis, and that they are legally and procedurally adequate.

When it comes to the conduct of cases, there may be differences in approach. Lawyers tend to place an emphasis on maximising areas of agreement with other parties and on settling, where possible, out of court (Dickens, 2005). Social workers may be suspicious of such an approach, believing that cases are only brought when normal, cooperative working has already failed and that compromise settlements may leave children vulnerable. Note that the introduction in England and Wales, from April 2008, of *The Public Law Outline* (PLO) (Ministry of Justice and Judiciary of England and Wales, 2008) moves this argument firmly in favour of the lawyers' aim of maximising agreement. One important feature of the PLO is the use of advocates' meetings, where lawyers meet without any of their clients, in order to achieve agreed outcomes where possible, and otherwise to narrow down the areas of disagreement upon which the court will be asked to adjudicate. There is an explicit intention of reducing the length and the cost of proceedings.

Lawyers may also be reluctant to fight weak cases because of the risk of misleading the court and thus damaging their own and the local authority's reputation (Dickens, 2005). Yet social workers continue to believe that lawyers have an additional responsibility to present weaker cases as strongly as possible.

So how can social workers and lawyers work together? Consider the following case example.

Case example 6.1a

A series of agency social workers has been involved with the Perkins family over the past three years in response to several referrals from teachers and health visitors expressing serious concerns for each of Jane Perkins' three children. Jane is a 26-year old white British single parent living in England. There have been child protection conferences and a child protection plan is in place, reflecting concerns about neglect. The newly allocated local authority social worker has been working with the family following a fire that has made the front room of the house uninhabitable. The fire appears to have been caused by large amounts of washing hung over a nursery fireguard. Because of the damage to the house, Jane has agreed to the children being accommodated temporarily with local foster carers, under s.20 of the Children Act 1989. However, the new social worker and her manager have concluded that the serious and prolonged nature of the concerns for the children, combined with the lack of progress, means that the local authority should also consider the need to start care proceedings. This is the recommendation of the most recent review case conference.

Case example 6.1 will be expanded throughout this chapter. It relates to an application for a care order under s.31 of the Children Act 1989. It has long been the case that local authorities would take legal advice before making an application to the court. But, since the introduction of the PLO and the revision of Volume 1 of the Children Act 1989 Guidance Regulations (Department for Children, Schools and Families, 2008), there is now a clear process whereby, in non-urgent cases, lawyers and social workers together must ensure that various tasks are carried out before making an application to the court. These tasks include:

- carrying out a core assessment under the Framework for Assessment (Department of Health, 2000b)
- considering alternative kinship options
- writing to the family (a 'letter before proceedings') outlining the local authorities' concerns and explaining what the family should do if proceedings are to be avoided.

In this case the social worker and her manager set up a meeting with the local authority lawyer. In the language of the PLO and of Volume 1 Children Act Guidance, this may be referred to as a 'legal gateway meeting'. This meeting does not involve the family. The key purposes are to decide whether or not any significant harm that has happened or is likely to happen to the children meets the threshold criteria under s.31 of the Children Act 1989 and, if so, whether a letter should be sent to the parents before the proceedings.

Note that in this case the social worker and her manager are suggesting care proceedings. In order to get good legal advice at the gateway meeting, the social worker should make available much of the case material, particularly an up-to-date chronology, a genogram, an up-to-date core assessment and any other relevant assessments.

This material might suggest alternatives to taking legal proceedings, or at least preliminary steps such as updating the core assessment, obtaining specialist assessments or holding a family meeting or Family Group Conference to consider whether the wider family might be able to help with resolving the local authorities' concerns or even, in some circumstances, might care for the children themselves.

In this case the meeting identified the following evidence, which might demonstrate that the threshold criteria in s.31 of the Children Act 1989 are met:

Case example 6.1b

- Jenny, who is 9 years old and white, was described by her schoolteachers as dirty and hungry – the social worker saw her eating frozen peas from the freezer. Jane said: 'She likes frozen food.'
- Danny, who is 3 and of mixed race, has a speech delay and has not been attending medical appointments.
- Joel, 5 is Danny's full sibling. He has not had had any immunisations and, according to health visitor assessment, has a global developmental delay. He has missed the last three appointments for his squint.
- There is a lack of cooperation from Jane: the last time the social worker helped her to take Joel to the GP she swore at the doctor and stormed out.
- After the fire, the house is in very poor condition.

For the purposes of this discussion, we are not really concerned about whether or not this evidence actually meets the threshold, or about whether or not making an application to court would be necessary to safeguard and promote the children's welfare. In reality, such judgements require far more detail than can be provided in this kind of case study and should include those made by people with first-hand experience of working with the family. Decisions about when to go to court in cases of chronic neglect are very difficult (Gardner, 2008), and this particular case may appear not to be clear-cut. However, the purpose here is to clarify how social workers, managers and lawyers work together to make such decisions. The point is that legal judgements about the quality of the evidence are closely intertwined with social work judgements about whether to go to court to try to safeguard and promote the children's welfare. And lawyers' concerns about the need to follow the correct procedures under the PLO and Volume 1 Children Act Guidance are closely intertwined with social workers' concerns about how best to manage the case. In this way lawyers and managers both carry some responsibility for case management. What is needed for a good working relationship between lawyers, social workers and their managers is a detailed understanding of each other's roles.

Even with a good mutual understanding, there is the possibility that a social worker may disagree with the stance taken by her manager. What happens if she is directed to start care proceedings but doesn't believe that this is necessary? As an employee, she has to take instructions; but as a professional she has a duty to the court to tell the truth on oath and to give her honest opinion. This means that, as soon as the social worker finds herself in this position, she must tell her lawyer about it. Giving evidence that contradicts the local authority's position without giving any warning is not acceptable. Note that this means that it is difficult for a local authority to make a case in court without the support of the social worker involved.

Skill summary: Working with legal advice

Developing a close working relationship with your lawyer is of critical importance when cases go to court. Whilst it may seem obvious that lawyers advise about evidence and procedure and social workers and their managers decide what to do, nonetheless there is considerable complexity and even some overlap in roles. Strategies for skilled working include:

* gaining a detailed understanding of the lawyer's role
* keeping the lawyer informed immediately about significant events
* understanding the rules about evidence and about court procedures
* building constructive personal relationships.

Learning this skill will help you to meet the following National Occupational Standards:

Key Role 3: Unit 11.
Key Role 4: Unit 12.
Key Role 5: Unit 16 and Unit 17.
Key Role 6: Unit 20.

Preparing Reports for Court

Before considering the style and content of reports for court, it is necessary to understand the role that written reports play within the court process. Judges or magistrates read written reports before the hearing starts and before anyone gives evidence in person. A well-presented written case can be highly persuasive and will get the social worker off to a good start.

Courts have access to a large number of case documents, and only a small proportion of them will have been written specifically for the court proceedings. The court is likely to see relevant case documents that predate the start of the proceedings, such as initial and core assessments, or plans for services to children in need. This means that such documents should match the style, quality, and line of argument contained in reports written with the court in mind. Given that it is not possible to predict with any accuracy which cases may go to court, this is another powerful reason why case recording and case files should always be maintained to a high standard and on time.

Under the terms of the PLO, documents that must be prepared by the social worker for the court include the social work statement and the care plan or interim care plan. Other documents that may already be held by the local authority and that, if so, must be filed (delivered to the court) include:

- social work chronology (an essential feature of every case file, to be updated throughout the proceedings)
- initial/core assessment
- section 7 and 37 reports
- material relating to relatives and friends (e.g. a genogram)
- any inter-agency material
- records of discussions with the family
- minutes of key meetings (e.g. strategy discussion record)
- pre-existing care plans (e.g. child protection plan)
- letter before proceedings
- other relevant pre-proceedings documents.

Court hearings are restricted to matters that the parties cannot agree on, or about which there is room for argument. A case that is soundly based and well presented on paper is likely to reduce the areas of disagreement for the court to hear and decide about, and it may even lead to an agreed settlement.

General questions of style

Even though reports are written for the court, a number of different people may read a court report for quite different purposes. First, there is the professional audience of lawyers for all the parties (that of the local authority, of the parents, of the Children's Guardian and sometimes of other family members). These people will be looking mainly for strengths and weaknesses in the social work case. Then there is the Children's Guardian, who will be analysing the social work case from a professional perspective, and the judge or magistrates, who will be looking for evidence and for reasoning in relation to the possible outcomes under the law. But, second, there is the audience of those personally involved in the case, both parents and children. Parents will be reading about themselves and, inevitably, about their failings. Children and young people may either read the report at the time, if they are old enough to take part in the proceedings, or perhaps later, when they try to find out what happened. This means that such reports have an impact not only on the conduct of the case in court, but also on the relationship between the social worker and the family, both in the short and in the long term.

Careful attention must be paid to tone and to language. In this book most of the case examples refer to people by their first names, because this reflects the kind of mutually acceptable language practice that typically exists between social workers and those with whom they work, even in statutory contexts. However, full names should be used in court reports, such as 'Mrs Jane Perkins' in our example, and people should not be referred to as 'the mother' or 'the father'. It is necessary to take care over names and to make sure that they are spelt and used correctly. It is clearly necessary to write about the causes of concern for the child. Because of the requirement to demonstrate that significant harm is due to parental care 'not being what it would be reasonable to expect a parent to give' (s.31(2) Children Act 1989), this report must include criticism of parents. However, emotive language should be avoided. So Mrs Perkins' house should not be described as 'filthy', and eating frozen peas directly from the freezer should not be described as 'disgusting'. Factual language should be used to explain what was observed, and the court will then be able to draw its own conclusion.

Care proceedings are adversarial in the sense that disagreements between parties are tested in court. But the tone of the social work report should be fair-minded in its approach to the evidence and sensitive to the parents' position. In many cases, particularly where the social worker has worked with the family for some time, there may be feelings of regret, sadness, or sympathy for parents who are failing to give reasonable care, even after attempts to help. It may be appropriate to acknowledge this in the report. Doing so may help future relations with parents, whether or not there is any plan to return the children to their care. It may also help to convince the court that past attempts to help have been genuine and that the current recommendations are reliable.

The tone of the social work report says a lot about the individual worker and about the approach to the work. This is illustrated in exercise 6.1.

Exercise 6.1

Consider the following ways of describing the problem in Case Example 6.1 of getting Joel seen by his GP:

1 Mrs Perkins is disorganised and finds it difficult to plan ahead. After three missed appointments I had to take her to the GP myself, but her poor impulse control meant that she swore at the GP and left before Joel was seen.
2 Mrs Perkins did not have any easy way of taking Joel to see his GP, so after three missed appointments I drove them there myself. Unfortunately, she became angry about the length of the wait and I was later told by the receptionist that she had sworn at the doctor and left the building without keeping the appointment.

Which do you think reflects good practice and why?

The first of the above descriptions starts with a negative judgement about Mrs Perkins, without evidence to support it. It then uses this judgement to explain the need for the social worker's intervention (the frustration at having had to take Mrs Perkins to the GP is barely hidden) and finally it lapses into jargon (poor impulse control) to give further evidence of Mrs Perkins' failings. The second is much more sympathetic in tone, implicitly acknowledging travel difficulties and providing some context for the angry outburst.

The two examples also differ in the way in which they deal with fact, analysis and opinion. In the first case, 'Mrs Perkins is disorganised and finds it difficult to plan ahead' is presented as a fact. But what happens if this is disputed, as any lawyer for Mrs Perkins would surely do? How can it be proved? Perhaps the failure to keep Joel's GP appointments is evidence in favour of this assertion. But, alternatively, the failure might be due to the lack of a car and a difficult bus journey. This first case uses an unproven assertion, presented as fact, to explain inadequate parental behaviour, thus confusing fact, analysis and opinion.

Good practice is to provide all three, but to separate them as far as possible. Social workers are seen as expert witnesses. They are expected not just to present the facts, but to analyse them and to give opinions within the area of their own expertise (in care proceedings, this includes matters of general child care). It may sound obvious, but the analysis must treat the facts fairly and lead to sensible opinions and recommendations that will persuade the court. There will usually be a range of possible options, and it may be that the best option is not obvious or clear-cut. The social worker's report should address all of the options and weigh the advantages and disadvantages of each.

Specific considerations about content

This section deals with three documents that social workers will prepare for the court: the chronology, the social work statement and the care plan. The last two are written especially for the proceedings, whereas the chronology should already exist on the child's case file. However, in practice, many chronologies require further work before they can be submitted to the court, and they are updated throughout the proceedings.

The chronology is a succinct list of key events ordered by date. It is designed to give an overview of the case in a way that can be agreed by all the parties. The events themselves may be described and analysed in detail elsewhere (usually in the social worker's statement), and it is helpful to cross-reference between documents. The chronology should not include advice received from the social worker's own lawyer. In the Perkins case, the chronology could record the date of first referral, the dates of the initial child protection conference and reviews, the dates of missed GP appointments for Joel, the date of the house fire and so on.

The care plan is prepared for each individual child using a standard format given by Local Authority Circular LAC 99 (29) (Department of Health, 1999). It outlines what the local authority plans to do if the order is made. It contains five main sections, as follows:

1   overall aim
2   child's needs, including contact
3   views of others
4   placement details and timetable
5   management and support by the local authority.

The social work statement is the place to give detailed evidence and to provide analysis, opinion and recommendations. Social workers usually file at least two versions: an initial statement when the proceedings are started and a final version for the final hearing. The latter is likely to contain a higher proportion of analysis and argument, addressing all the written evidence that has been submitted by all the parties.

Davis (2007) provides a helpful guide to the questions that provide a structure for the social work statement:

- *Who are you?* What is your role and why should I listen to you? The social worker should give her full name, professional address, job title, qualifications and experience. A brief explanation of her specific role with the family is helpful, and perhaps an indication of how long she has spent with them, as a way of establishing how well she knows them.

- *What are you asking the court for?* This should be made clear at the outset, but the analysis and reasoning should be saved for later.

- *Whom is the case about?* This section includes basic factual details about the child, but it also gives a picture of the child as a person. Lawyers and judges are unlikely to meet the child, and so this kind of information is helpful.

- *Who are the child's parents and what is the family structure?* This section gives details of the child's parents and of those with parental responsibility. It should include absent fathers, with or without parental responsibility, and half-siblings. In complex cases, a family tree or genogram may help.

- *What harm do you say that this child is suffering, or likely to suffer?* This should be a concise summary of the concerns.

- *What is the evidence for your allegations?* This is the longest part of the social work statement. It should include detailed observations rather than the conclusions that were drawn from them. The evidence should be based on written notes that were made at the time things happened, not some time later. Even if these are only rough notes jotted down in the car outside the house straight after the visit, they should be retained. In our case example, the incident when Jenny raided the freezer for peas should be described, and the general claim that she is not properly fed should be avoided. Specific family interactions should be described instead of making general claims about attachment relationships. The focus should be on the most relevant material and matters that might be thought to be trivial should be excluded. Note that facts which do not support the local authority's position must also be included. For example, there may be earlier positive assessments of parenting, or examples of the child functioning well. These should be discussed with the local authority lawyer.

- *What are the family's strengths?* The court will expect a fair and balanced view of the family. Failure to provide it will almost certainly be revealed to the court in cross examination and will make the social worker look biased and selective.

- *What has the local authority done?* The court needs to hear about attempts to improve things for the child. This is where good-quality social work practice not only helps the child directly but also helps in making an application to court, should one become necessary. It strengthens the argument that a court order is really necessary, as it undermines the argument that more help might solve the problem. If the social work practice in question is flawed, then it is best to acknowledge the fact.

- *What is your professional opinion?* This is where the social worker explores the facts of the case, giving her analysis and using her expertise to help the court to interpret the evidence. In our example, this would be the time to offer the opinion that Jenny is not being fed properly, if the accumulated evidence makes that a credible position to take.

- *What statutory criteria should be applied?* This varies depending on which order is being sought but, in each case, the detailed criteria in the relevant sections of the legislation should be considered in turn.

- *What is your conclusion and recommendation?* This section contains the social workers' summing up. It makes links between the key evidence and the outcome that is sought. This section should make sense on its own, because many readers will turn to it in isolation.

Skill summary: Preparing reports for court

Well-prepared written reports are important in court proceedings, although they cannot cover up for deficiencies in other areas of social work practice. In care proceedings the key documents are the chronology, the care plan and the social work statement. It is the last one that contains detailed evidence, analysis, opinion and recommendation. Skilfully written reports will:

- use formal, but plain and clear language
- avoid emotive language
- demonstrate sensitivity to the family
- adopt a tone that conveys the desired impression of the writer as social worker
- separate, as far as possible, between fact, analysis and opinion
- present a fair and balanced view of the evidence
- make reasoned recommendations that fit with the criteria for the order that is sought.

Learning this skill will help you to meet the following National Occupational Standards:

Key Role 5: Unit 16.

Negotiating with Other Parties to the Proceedings

In the run-up to the hearing, the parties' lawyers are often in contact with one another, trying to improve their client's position. Negotiations over aspects of the case usually carry on right up until the start of the hearing itself. Social workers may find this disconcerting. From the social worker's perspective, it seems clear that she would not have begun care proceedings had she not felt it was absolutely necessary to obtain a care order, albeit as a last resort. So how can compromise deals with the parents' lawyers be in the child's best interests?

In fact, the reason for the prevalence of these kinds of full, or partially negotiated, settlements is that they can be in everyone's interests, including those of the child. One common development is for parents to concede some or all of the evidence in the run-up to the hearing, or sometimes even on the day of the hearing itself. This may be because at that final stage they realise that there is no possibility of new evidence or new experts to help their case. They may also meet, for the first time, an authoritative barrister who reinforces the unpalatable advice that their solicitor has been giving all along. But, although they are prepared to make some concessions, it may be the case that parents want to gain something in the process, and they may seek some concessions from the local authority in order to reach agreement. The question is about the nature of any such concessions, how they are arrived at, and whether they allow the local authority to meet its legal duties towards the child.

Case example 6.1c

The letter before proceedings was issued, but there was no change in Jane's position. Because of this, the local authority has applied for an interim care order in respect of all three children. (An interim care order protects the child until a final hearing can be arranged.) The children are still accommodated in foster care under s.20 of the Children Act 1989 and their mother, Jane, accepts that they should stay there until the final hearing, although she wants to see them regularly.

On the day of the court hearing Jane's solicitor proposes a deal: her client agrees to sign a written agreement, to be filed at court, undertaking that the children will remain in foster care. Further, Jane undertakes to work with the social worker to improve things for the children, starting with supervised contact with them and leading, in due course she hopes, to a plan for their return home. In these circumstances she suggests that the local authority does not need to seek an interim order. The children will be safe in foster care until the case can proceed to the final hearing.

Exercise 6.2

Make a list of the potential advantages and disadvantages to the local authority's case if it were to agree to the proposal from Jane Perkins' solicitor in case example 6.1c.

In the case example, Jane's solicitor wants to avoid the interim care order; to prevent the court from hearing evidence that might put Jane in a bad light at this early stage; to demonstrate that Jane is cooperative and has her children's interests at heart; and to improve Jane's position at the final hearing.

The tactics in negotiation with the local authority are to promise Jane's cooperation whilst reminding everyone that the local authority can return to court at short notice if needed and that the no-order principle under s.1(5) of the Children Act 1989 may apply.

How should the local authority respond? The most pressing need is for absolute clarity about why an interim order is needed. What exactly are the risks of significant harm that the local authority is concerned about, and why? What is the care plan? Is it to work towards a return home or not? If it is about a return home, then this negotiated deal may offer some advantages for the local authority. A tightly worded agreement could be enough to protect the children, given that the main concerns are about neglect. And a structured plan for contact, combined with some form of intervention with Jane, sounds very similar to the local authority's care plan. With the backing of the court the plan can be thoroughly tested, demonstrating the local authority's good faith. If it goes well, then that's great. If it does not, then there will be clear evidence to use in the final hearing. Either way, the children's interests are protected.

In practical terms, on the day of the hearing and before the case starts, the parties may be in separate rooms, with their solicitors moving backwards and forwards between them with revisions of proposals. In some courts it is common for discussions to take place in the corridor. The child's social worker will be involved in these discussions, alongside her lawyer. It is important to have anticipated the kinds of deals that may be offered and to have thought about possible responses in advance. However, even with good preparation, there may be some surprises on the day and the social worker may need to think quickly. It is important to know who within the local authority has the authority to reach agreement. Is it the social worker herself, her line manager, or another senior manager? Arrangements should be in place to contact any relevant person who is not at court.

Skill summary: Negotiating with other parties to the proceedings

In many cases lawyers will, quite properly, attempt to improve their client's position by negotiating with other parties, often on the day of the hearing. Social workers need to understand this process and, together with their lawyers, they must be prepared to respond. Skilled negotiation means:

- being clear about your desired goal and understanding the strengths and weaknesses of your case
- anticipating other parties' goals and strategies
- knowing what, under some circumstances, might be conceded and what cannot
- knowing the limits of your own authority.

Learning this skill will help you to meet the following National Occupational Standards:

Key Role 5: Unit 14.
Key Role 6: Unit 20.

Giving Oral Evidence

Evidence is presented to the court in the form of written reports. At the hearing itself the social worker will be expected to answer questions about that written evidence. Such questions will come, in turn, from the following parties.

- *The local authority's lawyer* This questioning is usually brief and serves to confirm that what has been said in writing is true. It can provide a verbal update if needed. This phase is known as 'giving evidence in chief.

- *Other parties' lawyers, in turn* This is where the social worker's evidence is tested on behalf of those who may hold an opposing view, in the process of cross-examination.

- *The local authority's lawyer again* In re-examination, the local authority's lawyer has an opportunity to help the social worker to clarify any questions raised in cross-examination and to try to counter any arguments that are unhelpful to the case.

In order to prepare for this phase of questioning, it is necessary to set aside time to read the various statements over again, and all the other reports that have been submitted. In the witness box there will be a 'bundle' (a file containing all these reports, with numbered pages). The best way to prepare for a final hearing is to borrow the whole of the court bundle from the local authority lawyer and read it. It is also necessary to read, know and perhaps reference the social work file with post-it notes.

Case files with detailed case notes are not normally taken into the witness box, but they should be in court with the lawyer in case the social worker is asked to refer to it.

Conduct in the witness box

Witnesses are expected to take the oath or a non-religious affirmation. They should speak out clearly and, of course, social workers should try to project an appropriate level of confidence, no matter how they are feeling.

In responding to questions from lawyers, it is usual to turn and give the answers to the judge, judges or magistrates, not to the lawyer who asked the question. This is not the way normal conversation works, and it may take some getting used to. However, it makes sense to direct the answers to the decision-makers. This procedure counters the control over the witness that lawyers gain from the process of questioning; it keeps the decision-makers engaged; and it may give the witness some clues as to how the evidence is being received.

Cross-examination

This is the crux of the matter and the process that witnesses, understandably, are most concerned about. But two of the key skills that are needed in withstanding cross-examination have already been considered. Since the objective is to expose flaws in the case, it is clear that skilled working with the lawyer to submit a well-prepared case is the fundamental key to success. Once in the witness box, social workers should continue to use the skills shown in their written reports by resorting to formal, but plain and clear language, by showing sensitivity to the family and by presenting a fair and balanced view of the evidence.

However, having an understanding of how lawyers approach cross-examination may also help. Factual evidence can be challenged by suggesting that the social worker's perception of events is incorrect; perhaps they misinterpreted what they saw? Alternative interpretations may be put. It may be suggested that the social worker's memory is incorrect, which is why accurate and timely record keeping is important. It may be suggested that the social worker is prejudiced against the lawyer's client, or even lying, although the latter should not be put to a professional witness without some evidence. When it comes to evidence of opinion, much hangs on the social worker's level of expertise and experience, particularly in comparison to that of other professionals (for example psychologists) who may be expressing different views. There isn't much that the social worker can do about this other than to be clear about the rationale for her views and to stick to them.

Cooper gives the following tips for responding to questions:

- If you are led to say something which you did not really mean or which gives the wrong impression, set the record straight immediately.
- Do not feel obliged to change your answer, if it is accurate, simply because you are asked the same question in a different form or repeatedly.

- Hold your ground where appropriate, but do not be afraid to concede a valid point made to you in cross-examination.
- Do not argue – it is the lawyer's job to test your evidence.
- Do not try to score points off the cross-examiner.
- Remember that your role is to assist the court in reaching the correct decision. (Cooper, 2006: 80)

Skill summary: Giving oral evidence

Giving evidence in relation to a weak or ill-prepared case can be a chastening experience. Preparing a strong case and presenting it in a fair and balanced way on paper is an essential precursor to doing the same thing in oral evidence. Skilled practice includes the following injunctions:

- Prepare by reading all the reports and by knowing the key arguments of your case.
- Show sensitivity to the family.
- Talk to the judge or judges in response to questions, not to the questioner.
- Be prepared to deal calmly with challenges to your position.
- If the judge or magistrates are making notes of your evidence, then watch the pen and don't rush the writer. If you speak too quickly, they may miss something important.
- Don't use jargon and keep it simple.

Learning this skill will help you to meet the following National Occupational Standards:

Key Role 3: Unit 11.
Key Role 5: Unit 16.

Managing Relationships with Service Users during and after Proceedings

Parents and families are likely to feel angry about the very fact that proceedings have started, and yet the social worker responsible may have to continue to work with them during and after the proceedings, despite their being on opposite sides. The social worker can't simply say 'See you in court!' and stop talking to them until the matter is resolved. So how should social workers approach the relationship during the proceedings?

There is an obvious need for sensitivity to families and to the distress that the court case causes them. Davis argues as follows:

In general, workers who are honest and clear with families throughout fare much better than those who tread too softly and do not confront the issues as they arise. Families can feel betrayed by a worker they thought was 'on their side' who then stands in court spelling out their failings in graphic detail. Equally, some sensitivity is required and being frank about problems does not mean that they have to be cruelly expressed. (Davis, 2007: 29)

Social workers must combine openness and honesty about their position with a demonstration of empathy for the position of the family. As we saw in Chapter 4, this is not easy but it is necessary for continued engagement with families.

After the case is concluded, assuming that the order is granted, a new set of issues comes into play. Someone has to tell the child, and also the parents if they were not in court. The social worker will need to talk to the guardian and the child's solicitor about who is in the best position to do this. In most cases, whilst the other professionals involved will never see the family again, either the original social worker or another one from the same local authority will continue to work with the parents after the hearing. Is a change of worker needed? Parents' initial reactions of raw emotion (such as refusing to have anything to do with the social worker, or with further plans for a child) are likely to change with time. Losses for parents following proceedings may be thought of as being similar to other losses (Currer, 2007).

Skill summary: Working with parents during and after proceedings

The significant thing here is that the adversarial nature of the proceedings makes it much harder to maintain a working relationship with the child's parents. Nonetheless, in most cases some form of contact with parents will continue throughout the proceedings. Skilled workers will:

- deal with anger and hostility
- present their concerns for the child straightforwardly
- show sensitivity to the parents' position.

Learning this skill will help you to meet the following National Occupational Standards:

Key Role 2: Unit 5.

Conclusion

For social workers committed to the principles of anti-oppressive practice, the decision to commence court proceedings may seem to be a kind of failure. If it represents a minimal intervention, then it is a very serious one, and the opportunities for empowerment and partnership are limited.

This altogether negative view of proceedings is balanced by the account of skills contained in this chapter. We must be very clear about the relationship between social work in statutory contexts and the aims and values of social work as a whole. As we saw in Chapter 2, statutory interventions, including court proceedings, are designed to protect vulnerable people and can represent a productive use of power. This means understanding the need to continue to work with opposing parties to the proceedings, respecting their rights, presenting a balanced view of their position and showing appropriate empathy. Whilst it may not be sensible to claim that this represents anti-oppressive practice as it is understood by some of its proponents, nonetheless the skilled court work described in this chapter can be understood as an appropriate application of the principles of anti-oppressive practice to the context of court work.

FURTHER READING

Cooper, P. (2006) *Reporting to Court under the Children Act: A Handbook for Social Services*, 2nd edn. London: TSO. A detailed, authoritative and accessible handbook covering the preparation of reports for court in relation to the Children Act 1989. Includes a section on giving oral evidence.

Davis, L. (2007) *See You in Court: A Social Worker's Guide to Presenting Evidence in Care Proceedings*. London: Jessica Kingsley Publishers. Covers both report writing and giving oral evidence.

Seymour, C. and Seymour, R. (2007) *Courtroom Skills for Social Workers*. Exeter: Learning Matters. An introductory text.

7

Skills for Promoting Change

Chapter summary

Skills for interventions are closely related to the skills for assessment and planning that were considered in Chapter 5. This chapter considers the skills needed for promoting change in statutory contexts, where the people involved may not want the change that the local authority seeks in order to carry out its legal duty. Is individual motivation to change a prerequisite? If so, how can it be understood? This chapter looks at the skills needed to promote motivation to change, to negotiate over what should be done and how, and to widen the intervention so as to include work with wider systems.

Consider the following situations:

1 Brian is on an intensive supervision and surveillance order (ISSO) with the aim of preventing reoffending.
2 Moses has been assessed at home by a psychiatrist and an approved social worker. The psychiatrist thinks he is suffering from acute depression and both agree that there is a risk of suicide and that there may be a need for compulsory hospital admission.
3 Mary and John have been sent a letter before proceedings outlining the changes they must make if the local authority is not to commence care proceedings under the Children Act 1989.

In each of these situations the role of the social worker is to promote change within a statutory context. In each case there is external pressure on the people involved, either to make changes or to risk a return to court, compulsory admission to hospital, or care proceedings. In Chapter 2 we considered some of the complex ethical issues that are raised by this kind of work. Why would social workers want to work in statutory contexts, and does such work fit with the aims and values of the profession? The current chapter moves on to consider how to promote change.

What methods of intervention may be used in statutory contexts? First we will consider those in use throughout the whole of social work. The following list is based on the work of Coulshed and Orme (2006) and of Walker and Beckett (2003).

- *Crisis intervention* Ideas from psychodynamic theory are used to help individuals to maximise the opportunity for change and to reach optimum levels of functioning after a crisis.

- *Systems intervention* Attention is paid to the social context of an individual, including: family, friends, support groups, professional systems.

- *Psychodynamic intervention* Theoretical ideas about the nature of the mind (e.g. defence mechanisms, transference) are used in order to help people to gain insight into their own behaviour.

- *Cognitive–behavioural intervention* This is a method for altering thinking, feeling and behaviour.

- *Task-centred intervention* Based on the person's agreement, this method seeks to move from problem to goal-setting. It is a short-term and a time-limited method.

- *Community work intervention* Rooted in social justice, such interventions aim to mobilise the collective strengths of people.

This is not the place for a full discussion of these interventions, and some further reading is included at the end of the chapter. The question here is the extent to which they, or any other methods of intervention, may be used to promote change in statutory contexts. Or, to put it differently: are there specific social work skills that are needed in order to use these interventions effectively in statutory contexts?

Motivation to Change

One of the key issues for social work interventions in statutory contexts is the question of people's motivation to change. There is a very old joke that goes like this: 'How many social workers does it take to change a light bulb?' Answer: 'Only one, but the light bulb must really want to change!' The joke may not be very funny, but it seems to go to the heart of the matter. If it captures something true, then the implication is that social work is limited to situations in which people actually want to change. From an ethical point of view, this may be entirely welcome; but where does it leave us in relation to work in statutory contexts where change may not be wanted, but may be required in order to fulfil the local authority's legal duty?

But, first, is it actually true that the interventions listed above require the person to want to change? Certainly they all require the informed consent of the person involved, and none of them is designed to be used in an overtly coercive context. Indeed, task-centred intervention is explicitly based on the idea that the persons themselves should identify the goals of the work. But none of these interventions requires that the person must come to the social worker with a clear commitment to resolving the problem. The literature on psychodynamic interventions, for example, pays much attention to the process of engaging the person in the work. In all these interventions, a helping relationship must be established (see Chapter 4), and this includes the process of reaching agreement about the goals and the nature of the intervention.

There is some evidence that this process is just as important in statutory contexts. For example, in the USA, coercive social work interventions are sometimes used in relation to offending and to substance misuse. Yatchmenoff (2008) records that such legal coercion leads to greater enrolment and attendance on, for example, substance abuse programmes, but that there are serious questions about whether this leads to significant change. Drawing on evidence from her own studies of engagement with child protective services in Oregon, Yatchmenoff argues

> that compliant behaviours [such as attending a programme] [. . .] are not a substitute for an internal state of engagement (that is, *a feeling state of positive involvement in a helping process*) and that this feeling state is one of the determinants of whether or not positive outcomes

are achieved [. . .] In one worker's words: 'If the client is not on board, you have nothing.' (Yatchmenoff, 2008: 62, original italics)

So it seems that, even in statutory contexts, the people involved must be on board before social work interventions can achieve positive outcomes.

But, as we have seen, in statutory contexts people may respond to unwanted contact from a social worker by feeling threatened, defensive or angry. In direct contrast with someone who phones a social worker asking for help, it seems unlikely that they will want help to change. This means that, in statutory contexts, the skills required to create and sustain a motivation to change are more important than ever. So what are these skills?

A model of change

Before we can answer these questions we need to understand something about how and why people may change their behaviour. One influential model has been developed by Prochaska and DiClemente (1982). This is a stage model describing how people may move out of addictive behaviours such as drug-taking. It describes a linear process, from pre-contemplation through contemplation to action and maintenance. However, the model recognises the likelihood of relapsing into old behaviours and suggests that a relapse may lead back to the earlier stage of contemplation. This makes the process of change circular or, more hopefully, an upwards spiral.

This model has been particularly influential in relation to social work practice in safeguarding children. Specifically, the Department of Health issued training materials to assist in the introduction of the Framework for the Assessment of Children in Need and their Families (Department of Health, 2000b). These materials include a chapter on assessing parental motivation to change (Horwath and Morrison, 2000) that draws heavily on Prochaska and DiClemente's (1982) model. In addition, Calder (2008) uses the model to develop a framework for working with resistance, motivation and change. At each stage it has been suggested by Calder that the worker may have a role to play in promoting change. Table 7.1 gives a summary of the model and of the possible roles for workers.

This model provides a useful way of thinking about the differences between the starting points of professionals and those they work with in statutory contexts. Whereas from the outset professionals may be ready for action, those involved are more likely to be at the

Table 7.1 Worker's role in Prochaska and DiClemente's (1982) model of change

Stage of change	Description	Possible role for worker
Pre-contemplation	The individual is not even considering the possibility of change. There may be 'reluctance', 'rebellion', 'resignation', or 'rationalisation' (DiClemente, 1991), but at this stage no change is possible.	To provide information and awareness of the nature of the problem and of the possibility of change.
Contemplation	During this phase the individual comes to accept that there is a problem and that they have some responsibility for it. They feel some discomfort and they come to see that things must, and indeed can, change. However, this is an ambivalent stage and change may still be rejected.	To try to tip the balance in favour of change (Miller and Rollnick, 1991). This may be one final external pressure, or it may be a positive incentive.
Action	The individual works to bring about the change.	To provide external support for change. To monitor progress.
Maintenance	Change is internalised, sustained and consolidated, no longer dependent on worker support. This is the desired end phase.	No role.
Relapse	The model recognises that the individual is unlikely to succeed first time around. Relapse is seen as a phase of change, often leading back to contemplation (or pre-contemplation).	Providing information about how change may include relapse. Providing encouragement.

SOURCE Based on Calder, M. (2008) 'A framework for working with resistance, motivation and change', in M. Calder (ed.), *The Carrot or the Stick? Towards Effective Practice With Involuntary Clients in Safeguarding Children Work*, pp. 120–40. Lyme Regis: Russell House Publishing.

pre-contemplation stage. This mismatch may have serious consequences unless the worker allows time for a move from pre-contemplation to contemplation and to action. The model may be helpful
in promoting a less pejorative view of people who are not ready to
change, and it may encourage greater patience.

Limitations of the model

Limitations fall into two categories. First it has been argued that there
are some limitations within the model itself. As with all stage theories,
it is argued that it imposes artificial categories onto what may be a
complex, continuous process, and that the idea of an orderly progression through discrete stages may be an oversimplification. Calder
(2008) gives an account of the evidence for these arguments. Second,
and more important for our purpose, comes a set of questions about
the validity of transferring a model from the field of addictive behaviours to statutory social work contexts, specifically in the areas of
parenting and safeguarding children.

Corden and Somerton (2004) discuss a number of these
questions:

- *Are addictive behaviours similar to other behaviours, particularly
  parenting behaviours?*   One feature of addictive behaviours may
  be that there is a direct physiological link between the behaviour
  and pleasurable changes in brain chemistry. Where this is the case,
  it may be particularly difficult to promote change through interpersonal or legal 'pressure'. Hence the need for personal motivation on the part of the individual. Corden and Somerton argue
  that parenting behaviours are better seen as learned behaviours,
  and that the same analysis does not necessarily apply.

- *Do all changes in parenting behaviour require contemplation?*   The suggestion here is that many changes in parenting
  behaviour occur without a conscious intention to change. For
  example, some years ago I took my young daughter regularly to
  a pre-school drop-in playgroup. I found that I learnt lots about
  young children, about play, and about communication with them
  as a result of watching and learning from others. But before going
  I was not aware of any deficit in me and I saw no need to change.
  I probably would have been offended and even resistant if anyone
  had suggested that I needed to change. There is a danger in using
  this model: pre-contemplative parents may be assessed as being

resistant to change when in fact they may be very open to it – provided they don't have to contemplate it first!

- *Is the concept of relapse appropriate in the context of safeguarding children?* In the context of safeguarding children, some of the starkest examples of relapse may present serious dangers (for example a relapse into sex offending in a man living with his family). But in most cases desired changes in parenting behaviour are likely to be small and incremental, unlike the all-or-nothing changes often associated with ending addiction. Relapse is arguably less relevant when dealing with a process of incremental change.

- *Does the model predict timescales for change that meet children's needs?* The concern here is that the stages themselves are defined by relatively long time periods (in the model, contemplation means considering change within three months) and the empirical data suggest that, with relapse, change can take much longer. If the desired change consists in stopping assaulting or neglecting a child, then change at this rate may not be acceptable in the context of meeting children's needs.

Social work has always been strongly influenced by ideas drawn from other disciplines. However, the above discussion demonstrates that such ideas should not be introduced uncritically. The starting point for this discussion of the model proposed by Prochaska and DiClemente (1982) was the claim that, if we are to consider skills for increasing motivation, then it would be helpful to understand something about how and why people change their behaviour. It seems that this model is helpful for understanding how people move away from addictions, but that there is a need for a better understanding of how people make changes in other areas of their lives.

Exercise 7.1

Think of some of the positive changes that have occurred in your life – for example, improvements in relationships, lifestyle changes, or new starts.

- Were these the result of a pre-planned decision to change?
- Does improvement vary depending on the type of change?
- Do the stages of pre-contemplation, contemplation and action apply?

Promoting the motivation to change

The discussion so far has begun to demonstrate some of the complexities of the topic. In order to move us closer to a consideration of social work skills, we will use a more detailed case example. Julie's story was introduced in Chapter 2 as case example 2.1, when we were considering the aims and ethics of social work in statutory contexts; but the story continues throughout the current chapter, as we consider the various types of social work interventions that took place.

Case example 7.1a

When social worker Melanie first met Julie Morris, Julie's baby was due in six weeks' time. That meeting is described in Chapter 2, but let us recap: Julie is a 27-year old white British woman from a disadvantaged background. Julie's three older children have been removed from her care and placed for adoption because of evidence of physical abuse and neglect. Julie has a history of being sexually abused as a child, of constantly running away from home and care placements, of self-harming, drug misuse and, as an adult, she has been diagnosed by a psychiatrist as having a borderline personality disorder.

At the first meeting with her new social worker Melanie, Julie was very angry and distressed about the removal of the three older children. She made it clear that she was convinced that the local authority would remove the new baby as soon as it was born. Melanie was able to reassure Julie that the agreed position of the local authority was that they would work to support Julie in safely caring for the new child, probably in the context of a child protection plan, rather than seeking a legal order for the baby's removal. This was a reflection of the local authority's view that there had already been signs of change in Julie's situation since the court case that had led to the removal of her older children some two years ago. These changes were:

- new and suitable housing
- a more stable pattern of mental health, with fewer admissions to hospital
- a report from Julie's current psychiatrist which tentatively linked the diagnosis of 'borderline personality disorder' to experiences of childhood trauma and suggested that Julie may be ready for some psychotherapeutic help
- signs of realistic preparations for life with the new baby.

Julie's mistrust of social workers was an obvious problem. Julie was very reluctant to meet with Melanie at all, and she was refusing to allow Melanie to visit her at home. Since home visiting would be a normal part of a child protection plan, this became an early test of their relationship. After discussion with her line manager, Melanie agreed to meet Julie at the office rather than at home, at least during this early stage of the work. In part, this reflected the fact that the physical condition of the house had not been a significant concern in the past. But, more importantly, it signalled to Julie that Melanie was willing to negotiate.

Melanie met with Julie several times during her pregnancy. At this early stage Melanie's main aim was to make sure that Julie actually wanted to make the changes that would be needed in order for her to keep the new baby safe and to demonstrate an acceptable degree of safety to the local authority. Melanie felt that Julie's motivation was the key. But Julie used these meetings to make her own position very clear to Melanie, as follows:

- Julie did not want the local authority to start care proceedings or to remove this new baby – she was committed to caring for the child.
- She saw previous social work interventions as entirely unhelpful, just adding to the pressure.
- The constant threat of legal action to remove the children had, in itself, been a reason for her mental health problems in the past.

Melanie emphasised their shared goal of Julie caring for her new child. She asked Julie for her views about the problems that she had encountered previously. Over a period of time Julie began to talk about the pressures of poor living conditions, unhelpful contact from her extended family, her lack of useful support and her mental ill health. She began to hint to Melanie that her childhood sexual abuse had been on her mind after the birth of the previous children.

What does the case study show about Julie's motivation to change, and about Melanie's role in promoting that motivation? There are a number of things to note:

1 The statutory context places an enormous amount of external pressure on Julie to change. The external motivators could hardly be greater. The message appears to be: change or else.
2 Julie finds this pressure almost intolerable and experiences its impact as entirely negative.
3 Julie's internal motivation is clear enough – she wants to care for her child.

4 Despite this shared overall goal of Julie caring safely for her child, there is no real agreement yet over what, if anything, needs to change.

From Melanie's perspective, the strategy was to emphasise the shared overall goal. In this respect Julie's motivation was not really in doubt. However, it was clear that to impose a list of non-negotiable detailed changes at this stage would not be helpful. Instead, Melanie patiently explored Julie's views about the previous difficulties, with a view to trying to identify a series of changes that would make sense to both of them, within the overall context of keeping the child safe.

Skill summary: Nurturing the motivation to change

Even in statutory contexts, the people involved must be 'on board' if social work interventions are to result in positive change. External pressure for change that derives directly from the statutory context is unlikely to be enough to motivate people to change. Indeed, resistance is a likely outcome. Skilled work in this area includes:

- being clear and honest about the overall aims of the intervention from the worker's perspective
- listening carefully to the perspective of the person involved
- exploring changes that make sense to that person
- negotiating over how these fit with the aims of the work in its statutory context
- being aware that positive change can occur even if the person does not understand the need for it and is not contemplating it.

Learning this skill will help you to meet the following National Occupational Standards:

Key Role 1: Unit 1.
Key Role 2: Unit 5 and Unit 9.
Key Role 4: Unit 12.

Negotiating over Interventions

It should be clear from the previous section that motivation is closely tied to questions about who is in control of the social work intervention and what they want to get out of it. Attempts to impose the agenda of the agency, without regard for the perspective of the person involved, are not so likely to achieve positive change as those that take account of that perspective. So this implies a process of negotiation similar to the one of negotiating over assessments that we considered in Chapter 5.

Negotiating with those involved over the aims and form of social work interventions is common to most social work settings. But in statutory contexts there are some distinctive dynamics that we will consider. These are illustrated in the unfolding of the case example of Julie Morris.

Case example 7.1b

Julie had a son whom she named Daniel. One of the key issues in social worker Melanie's mind was the question of what needed to change in order for Daniel to be safe. Rather than impose a list of required changes, Melanie decided to try to encourage Julie to identify areas in which she acknowledged the need for change and might accept some support. But when Melanie introduced this idea she found that Julie would not take the initiative. The message from Julie was that, although she had found things difficult at times when caring for the other children, nonetheless with Daniel things would be OK.

In supervision, Melanie thought about the reasons for this attitude. The obvious blocks were Julie's anger and distress about the previous legal action and her unwillingness to agree that it had been in any way necessary. But Melanie also came to suspect that there was a second problem.

Julie had been talking about her ongoing mental health problems and about the way in which a positive relationship with her current psychiatrist had enabled her to gain voluntary admission to hospital in times of crisis. However, Julie was insistent that she would not need this, or other support, in the future. She insisted that her problems were entirely resolved. Melanie suspected that Julie was worried that the local authority would not find this kind of intermittent hospital admission acceptable in the context of looking after a baby. What would happen to Daniel while Julie was in hospital? Julie might well think that this would be a trigger for legal action. More broadly, Melanie realised that Julie was unable to predict what level of support the local authority would consider legitimate for her as a parent, before deciding that she was not able to meet Daniel's needs. Refusing to accept the need for any help may just be a way of playing safe.

Because of Julie's apprehensions, Melanie realised that she needed to outline the local authority's position in greater detail. Without suggesting that she fully understood what Julie might need, nonetheless Melanie talked in general terms about the kind of supports that might be relevant. Crucially, because of the lack of family support, this included the possibility of providing short-break foster carers who might help out by looking after the baby during crisis hospital admissions and perhaps at other, planned, times. The key would be to provide a consistent pattern of care.

This discussion of possible support proved helpful in that it enabled Julie to be more open about her own perception of her needs. As a result, a child protection plan was agreed that included elements of support such as:

- provision of short-break foster care
- a volunteer home visitor from a local family support organisation, who would also act as a link with the foster carers
- attendance at a community drop-in support group for single parents.

In the months that followed, Julie used all of these supports. She formed a particularly strong relationship with the foster carers – a retired couple whom she came to treat rather like grandparents. Indeed, Julie came to see them as being on her side to such an extent that she did not want them to report back formally to the local authority or to attend the review case conference. Melanie found that Julie had tried hard to persuade the foster carers of her point of view; Melanie herself had to step in so as to ensure that everyone was clear about the statutory context for the work. Framed positively, such reporting back to the conference about progress was the means by which the local authority might be reassured that Daniel was safe and that there was no need to continue with the plan.

Barriers to accepting help

It may seem that the process of negotiating over what help may be needed is simply a case of somehow reconciling the professional views about what must change with the person's own views of what help is needed. But this may be an oversimplification.

This is because, in statutory contexts, people may not be in a position to be open and straightforward about their needs. The dilemma is often very stark. Imagine being in this position. If you are open about your need for help, then this may be construed as implying an inability to cope, which in turn may be construed as some form of fault or weakness. In a context where the local authority might use any such admission against you in court proceedings, this is the last thing you want to happen. Yet, on the other hand, you may be desperate for help. You may know that to try to manage without it runs the risk of what the local authority will regard as failure, perhaps giving grounds to start court proceedings anyway. So what should you do?

There should be no doubt that this is a dynamic that renders people relatively powerless and places them in a difficult dilemma. Consider the experiences of a group of women who had been attending a peer support group for mothers of sexually abused children. None of these women had ever been suspected of being involved in any way in the abuse of their children, although in some cases, unknown to the women, their male partner had been the perpetrator. In most cases there had been an enquiry under s.47 of the Children Act 1989, conducted in tandem with a police investigation. In every case the local authority had ended its involvement as soon as it had become clear that, because of the women's actions, there was no continuing risk to the children, and in some cases there was a successful prosecution. Many of the women had assured their social workers that they were coping well and did not need any help.

However, in the context of research interviews, the women were able to explain that this had not really been the case, and one gave the following explanation:

> I could never say to any of the social workers, as much as I liked them, how I really felt. I felt that if they thought that I had questioned my own ability as a mother then perhaps I must be guilty somehow. I felt like I had a role to play and that was to keep the family together and to keep the family together I had to play their game of being a good mother and excluding (the abuser) from the family in every way that they would suggest. It came naturally anyway, but if they had said, 'right you must move house', I would have moved house. I just followed their lead, I played their game, but it certainly didn't mean that they knew how I felt. They didn't know anything about how difficult life was, you know, as far as they were concerned, yes it was a difficult time but we were handling it very well. (Hill, 2001: 381)

This quote comes from a woman who was also a foster carer and who understood the child protection system. As she said elsewhere, she knew full well that there was absolutely no reason whatsoever for the local authority to start court proceedings, and no possible grounds for such action. Yet even she was worried about revealing the extent of her difficulties, for fear of being seen as a failing parent.

If this is the case for the woman in this research study, then imagine the situation for Julie in our case study. She has already had three children removed from her care. Talking to her social worker about what she might need in order to be successful as a parent could therefore be seen as playing with fire. Arguably, as Melanie realised, Julie might be more confident about accepting help if she knew more about the local authority's attitude towards the provision of help.

What help is legitimate?

We have arrived at the question of what help is legitimate because we have been thinking, from Julie's perspective, about the kind of change she might be able to sign up to. In the absence of family or friends to help out, if she asks for short breaks from caring for Daniel, will this be seen as a legitimate need or as evidence of a lack of commitment to him?

This specific question is part of a wider debate about the use of foster placements. Often these are reserved for situations in which families are unable to care for their children, even if the inability is felt to be temporary, and as such their use can be seen as a kind of failure. It has been argued that they have much more potential to be used in a planned and routine way to support families in caring for their children, without the implication of failure (Brown et al., 2005).

Exercise 7.2

Imagine that you are Julie's social worker. You are due to make an agreement with her about the use of support foster care placements for Daniel. There are two issues for you to consider:

1   the purpose of specific placements
2   their duration and frequency.

Make a list of the factors that you would take into account when deciding what purpose, duration and frequency to agree to.

We have already seen that, because of the fear of negative inferences, Julie is unlikely to ask for this kind of help. This puts the onus on the social worker to think through what kind of help would fit with the objectives of keeping Daniel safe and of enabling Julie to meet his needs, and to suggest it to Julie. But constructing and implementing a professional solution runs counter to the aim of negotiating with Julie an intervention that she is committed to. There is no easy answer to this problem, and suggesting alternatives to Julie is probably the best approach.

Limits to negotiation over interventions

Another distinctive feature of negotiating over interventions in statutory contexts is that the context itself may set some limits on what can be agreed. In Chapter 4 we noted the importance of being open from the outset about what these limits are. But during the work it may turn out that there are unexpected challenges to respond to.

In the case example, Julie wanted to keep the support foster carers out of the formal safeguarding procedures by asking them not to report back to the social worker, Melanie, and not to attend the review case conference. When Melanie asked Julie about this, Julie explained that she wanted to be able to trust the foster carers, and that she would not be able to do so if she thought that they were part of a monitoring process that might, if circumstances changed, provide evidence for court proceedings. From the local authority's point of view this was not acceptable, since the support foster care was part of a formal child protection plan. Melanie found that she had to make this position very clear to all the parties involved. However, this issue could equally well be looked at positively, insofar as evidence of progress from the foster carers would be needed as part of the evidence that might end the formal child protection plan. Melanie was able to soften the impact of this very clear 'No' by positively reframing the issue in this way.

Skill summary: Negotiating over interventions

In statutory contexts people may not be free to be open about the help they may need, for fear of negative consequences. In addition, they may not know what is available, or what levels of support the local authority might consider legitimate. These dynamics are inherently disempowering. In order to counter this, and in order to arrive at interventions that those involved can sign up to in a meaningful way, skilled negotiation may include the following strategies:

- being clear about the kinds of help that may be available
- suggesting possibilities
- being clear about the local authority's attitude towards particular kinds and levels of support
- maintaining clarity about the limits of the statutory context.

Learning this skill will help you to meet the following National Occupational Standards:

Key Role 2: Unit 5 and Unit 6.
Key Role 4: Unit 12.

Thinking Systemically

As we noted in Chapter 2, individual casework is sometimes criticised for the way in which it individualises human problems. It encourages professionals to focus on the relationship between the worker and the individual concerned because, in the broad family of psycho-dynamic interventions, this relationship is seen as the main way in which change occurs. However, it may be that this approach exaggerates the significance of the social worker's efforts.

Alternative ways of thinking and intervening draw on systems theory. Here we are not thinking about family systems approaches (where an understanding of how all the individual members of a family can influence one another is the key to a variety of therapeutic interventions), but about the approach advocated, for example, in an influential book by Pincus and Minahan (1973). These authors argued that people are involved in 'systems' such as the family, the community, schools and work, and that these systems are of such significance for satisfactory functioning that they should be taken into account in attempts to help. Efforts to promote change should not be restricted to the relationship between the individual and the worker, but should be targeted on significant elements of these wider systems.

Note that these ideas are related to the concept of networks (Trevillion, 1992) and to the kind of ecological approaches that underpin the current Framework for the Assessment of Children in Need and their Families (Seden, 2001).

The question for the current chapter is, as ever, that of the application of these ideas to social work in statutory contexts. Is it possible to broaden the focus of intervention beyond the individual, when the context for the work is statutory? It is time to return to our extended case study in order to illustrate some of the issues.

Case example 7.1c

In the first few months Julie was able to maintain a consistent pattern of physical and emotional care for Daniel, with the support of midwives and health visitors at first and, later, of support foster carers and a volunteer home visitor. However, after a while things became more difficult.

Julie began to talk to Melanie about her relationship with her family, who had found out about the birth. As a teenager in care, having run away from home, Julie had told professional staff how her father sexually abused her when she was a child. She had not made a formal complaint to the police and he had never been prosecuted. Julie's mother never believed her. One of the perceived advantages of the recent move to a new house was that it gave her a physical separation of several miles from what was quite a large extended family. Now that Daniel is six months old, Julie has told Melanie that she is worried because her father is insisting on seeing Daniel and this is increasingly on her mind. Julie says that she is confident he will not harm a baby, but she does not know what to do. In the longer term she is wondering about the possibility of having some counselling.

Until now Julie had refused point blank to talk to Melanie about her family, saying that she had no contact with them. However, this conversation revealed that Julie had been talking recently to her older sister, Donna, who had two small children. Donna had recently fallen out with the rest of the family, having been openly critical of the way in which her parents were treating her own children.

Sensing a potential ally for Julie, and with her agreement, Melanie went to talk to Donna. This meeting proved to be a significant turning point. First, Donna was very open and angry about the physical and sexual abuse she had suffered during her childhood and had only begun to talk about recently. Second, she had started attending a support group for women survivors of abuse. Third, she was sympathetic to Julie, whom she had not seen for several years, and she wanted to explore ways in which the two might support each other. Over several months this led to significant changes in the pattern of support for Julie and Daniel:

- Julie began to attend the support group with Donna.
- She began to have individual psychotherapy arranged by her psychiatrist.
- Donna began to work with the support foster carers to care for Daniel when this work was at its most stressful for Julie.
- Julie and Donna were able to prevent their father from seeing any of the children.

Donna's involvement represented quite a big change in thinking for everyone. Until this point, both Julie and Melanie had felt that they were to some extent on their own. Melanie had felt a responsibility to find the solutions and to promote the changes needed to keep Daniel safe. Julie had felt that she could not trust Melanie, as was shown by her not wanting the foster carers to report back to Melanie.

It felt like a battle between the two of them. When Donna became involved, Julie's difficulties were more clearly seen in their family and social setting. Problems, solutions and responsibility for the care and protection of all three children became rather more shared. The two sisters also gained access to a lot of informal support from women in the group. They began to understand child sexual abuse differently, as an oppressive act and an abuse of power by the men involved rather than as something they, the sisters, were responsible for. Melanie continued to exercise authority by representing the need to demonstrate to the local authority that Daniel was safe; but the task of working out how to do this was one that Julie began to take increasing responsibility for, with support from her sister and from the survivors' group. Melanie began to see herself as less of an expert who should provide the solutions and more of a facilitator of solutions from within Julie's developing support network.

Skill summary: Going beyond a focus on individual change

There are real advantages to moving beyond a focus on the social worker's ability to promote individual change. There is a danger that such a narrow focus might get bogged down in anger, opposition to authority and apparent resistance to change. However, by focusing on the relationship between the naturally occurring networks around the child and the child protection system, there may be more opportunities for working anti-oppressively and for finding constructive solutions. Strategies for skilled interventions include:

- recognising and building on the strengths of the individual's network
- showing empathy
- not imposing expert solutions but facilitating change within the network
- encouraging an understanding of the experiences of oppression that may limit people's choices
- using authority to maintain the boundaries that are set by the statutory context.

Learning this skill will help you to meet the following National Occupational Standards:

Key Role 2: Unit 7 and Unit 8.

Conclusion

The skills needed for negotiation over statutory interventions are similar to those discussed in Chapter 5 in relation to assessments. In both cases skilled workers will seek opportunities to maximise the degree of choice and control exercised by those involved, but they will do so within the boundaries imposed by the statutory context. The skilled promotion of motivation to change is a key factor, but in some circumstances change may occur without an explicit commitment to it. Statutory contexts are those in which people are least free to ask for help; people may be disempowered by the fear that social workers would draw negative conclusions about them. Empowering practice takes this into account by making clear what legitimate support is available. Finally, skilled interventions look beyond the individual casework relationship to draw on structural understandings of oppression and on the individual's wider support networks.

FURTHER READING

Coulshed, V. and Orme, J. (2006) *Social Work Practice: An Introduction*, 4th edn. Basingstoke: Palgrave Macmillan. Part II outlines a number of methods of intervention.

Pincus, A. and Minahan, A. (1973) *Social Work Practice: Model and Method.* Itasca, IL: F. E. Peacock. Classic description of systems thinking and its application to social work.

Turnell, A., Lohrbach, S. and Curran, S. (2008) 'Working with involuntary clients in child protection: Lessons from successful practice', in Calder, M. (ed.), *The Carrot or the Stick? Towards Effective Practice with Involuntary Clients in Safeguarding Children Work*, pp. 104–15. Lyme Regis: Russell House Publishing. A context-specific account.

Wilson, K., Ruch, G., Lymbery, M. and Cooper, A. (2008) *Social Work: An Introduction to Contemporary Practice.* Harlow: Pearson. Chapter 11 on planning and intervention gives a helpful account of methods of intervention.

8

Ending, Evaluating and Reflective Practice

Chapter summary

This chapter considers the skills that are required to manage endings well and to evaluate and learn from the work that has been done. A consideration of evaluation and learning links to a final section about reflective practice. It moves away from the specific topic of endings and returns to questions that have run right through the book. What are the aims of statutory interventions? Whom are they for, and what are they trying to achieve? What does it mean to do the work skilfully, and what does anti-oppressive practice look like in statutory contexts? Only when we are clear about the answers to these questions can we begin to reflect on successes and failures.

In busy social work offices there is always pressure on workers to finish existing work and to move on to the next case. Sometimes it feels as though throughput is everything. In this context, the fact that one piece of work is coming to an end may be completely overshadowed by the next crisis situation, which is demanding urgent attention. And this lack of attention to the skills required during the ending phase of work appears to be matched by the relative lack of attention paid to the topic in the literature.

There are two reasons why this may be a problem. First, there is a significant group of people who may be re-referred to statutory social work teams because of changing circumstances that bring new or recurring difficulties or concerns. Problems caused, at least in part, by the experience of unsatisfactory endings can make it more difficult for them to re-engage in work. Second, the ending phase of the work is an obvious time to ask what has been achieved; what worked well, what went badly, and what can be learnt for future work. We need to make the most of opportunities for evaluating work and for learning from it.

Skills for Managing Endings

Social work interventions may come to an end in various ways. The most obvious divisions are between planned and unplanned endings, and between those endings agreed by everyone involved and those that are brought about by just one party. At first glance it might seem that planned and mutually agreed endings represent the most skilled practice; but, particularly in statutory contexts, this may not necessarily be the case. When there are contests over who is in control of the work, a unilateral decision to end it can be the most powerful way of taking control, particularly when this is done by someone who has been on the receiving end of the intervention. Sometimes work can be brought to an end for reasons that are unexpected or beyond anyone's control, and there is no simple correlation between the degree of planning that goes into endings and the degree of perceived overall success.

Endings and the concept of loss

From a psychodynamic perspective, the ending of a helping relationship can be understood as a kind of loss. Attachment theory provides a theoretical basis for this. In attachment theory, children's desire for physical and emotional closeness (attachment) to a particular carer (primary attachment figure) is seen as a primary motivational system (Bowlby, 1973). Being temporarily separated from a carer at a young age produces anxiety. This anxiety is then echoed in adulthood when we experience loss or separation from people who are important to us, most particularly when they die.

The following are commonly seen as significant stages in people's reactions to bereavement:

- *Emotional numbing and denial* At this stage feelings are too intense and cannot be tolerated.

- *Yearning, searching, anger* At this stage the bereaved person may continue to hope for the return of a loved one and become angry at anyone involved in the loss, including the dead person.

- *Disorganisation and despair* This results from the loss of the 'secure base' that attachment theory describes. In other words, the very person to whom the bereaved would have turned to for comfort is the one who is no longer there.

- *Reorganisation and resolution* Most people are able to readjust to such losses over time and to form new attachment relationships, although the pain of past losses continues to be felt. (Holmes, 1993)

In social work, these ideas about loss and people's reactions to it are widely seen as having an application beyond the experience of bereavement (Currer, 2007). As Wilson and colleagues note:

> Social workers need to be alert to the possible involvement of grief reactions, and responses to loss of many kinds, in their work. In effect, people may be profoundly 'attached' to all kinds of aspects of their lives apart from just loved ones – their home, their country, their job, their neighbourhood – and the loss of any of these can induce something akin to mourning. (Wilson et al., 2008: 581)

The question is: are these reactions relevant to the ending, or loss, of a helping relationship? Within the fields of psychotherapy and counselling, much attention has been paid to endings and to the losses involved for both parties (see, for example, Murdin, 2000). By way of contrast, within social work there is a comparative dearth of literature about the ending of social work interventions (Walker and Beckett, 2003).

One possible reason for this is the prevalence in social work of statutory contexts. After all, if social work help wasn't asked for in the first place, then its ending probably won't be experienced as a loss, but quite the reverse. People may be all too glad to get rid of the social worker and may have been working to that end. It seems likely that an acute awareness of this dynamic may lead social workers away from an understanding of endings in terms of loss.

But, as we have seen in previous chapters, even in statutory contexts that involve the use of authority, there can be meaningful engagement with people that leads to positive change. In these circumstances there may be complex feelings about the ending of the work, including perhaps a sense of loss. People may still feel angry about the intervention, yet fearful and uncertain about the future, now that the intervention is ending. Workers can feel guilty about leaving the situation, or frustrated about things they were unable to change. Consider the continuing case example of work with Darren.

Case example 8.1

In Chapter 4 we saw how Darren, who is 15 years old, was made subject to a referral order under the Youth Justice and Criminal Evidence Act 1999. He had assaulted another young person. He was living in a hostel for homeless young people, having fallen out with both parents. Darren's mother is white and English, and his father is black and born in Nigeria. Both have new partners with whom they have had children.

At the referral panel meeting, a contract was agreed to reduce the risk of Darren reoffending. It included the following elements:

- Darren's regular meetings with his social worker, Janet, to talk about how his behaviour has affected his mother, with whom he wishes to live
- anger management sessions, both in a group setting and individually with his social worker
- sessions with a drugs worker to consider the part that drugs and alcohol have played in his offending.

The order has now expired and the work has come to an end. Darren has mixed feelings. On the one hand he is glad to see the back of the Youth Offending Team and all the court pressures; but on the other hand he is concerned about the prospect of having to manage on his own, and he has enjoyed some of the sessions with his social worker, Janet. For her part, Janet is convinced that the intervention has reduced the risk of reoffending. Darren has understood the impact of his behaviour on others and is showing a more mature attitude. But he is still living in the hostel and things have improved a little, between him and his mother in particular. There are signs that he may be able to return home, but no promises have been made. Darren remains angry at times.

This case study reflects the sort of mixed feelings that are often present at the ending of statutory interventions, even when these endings are predictable and planned.

Coulshed and Orme (2006) suggest a model for ending that pays heed to some of these dynamics. Although seemingly not written with statutory contexts specifically in mind, nonetheless it contains useful pointers for such practice.

- Ending should be discussed at the first meeting, in the context of clarifying goals for the work.
- Ending should be used to underline what has been achieved, emphasising self-confidence and self-reliance.
- Fixed time limits for ending are often helpful in themselves.
- Allow time to explore feelings about an approaching ending.
- If there is to be a new worker, then introduce them.
- Help the person to build an informal helping network in the community.
- Be open about your own feelings about the ending.
- In some contexts, a 'ritual' ending may be appropriate (for example a party following the adoption of a child).
- Write a closing record together. (Coulshed and Orme, 2006: 287–8)

Unplanned endings throw up many of the same dynamics, but often in more unpredictable and perhaps more intense ways. Consider the outcome of the following case example, first introduced in Chapter 4.

Case example 8.2

An approved social worker, Michael, signed an application for a woman called Mary to be admitted to hospital for assessment under section 2 of the Mental Health Act 1983. Mary had been diagnosed by a psychiatrist as suffering from a mental illness and she had recently taken a serious overdose of prescribed drugs. Mary successfully appealed to a mental health review tribunal and subsequently refused any help following her return home. Some two weeks later she set fire to her flat. Fortunately no one was hurt, although extensive damage was done to the property. Michael heard that Mary has been compulsorily readmitted to hospital.

This may seem to be quite an extreme example, but it serves to remind us that not all statutory social work interventions are fully successful. Situations with poor outcomes, for whatever reason, are a significant part of the picture. We should be realistic about the limitations of social work in statutory contexts. Skills for managing and for getting the best out of less-than-ideal endings are also important.

One aspect of this case concerns dealing with how workers feel about poor outcomes. Supervision should provide an opportunity for

Michael to explore his feelings about the outcome of his work with Mary. He may well feel angry and frustrated that the review tribunal made what now appears to be the wrong decision. There may be lessons for him and for the agency to learn, for example about how the evidence was presented to the tribunal, and Michael may even feel guilty about his part in that process. However, Michael is no longer working with Mary, and because of this the opportunity for such a discussion may not arise, since supervision is typically focused on open cases. This seems to be a systematic flaw in the casework system, whereby lessons may not be learned from cases that have already been closed. The focus moves instead to the next urgent new case.

Skill summary: Managing endings

The circumstances in which social work in statutory contexts may come to an end are very diverse. Insights from attachment theory relating to the experience of loss suggest that the emotional dynamics of ending a helping relationship may be important. However, in statutory contexts things are complex. It is possible that the ending may not be experienced as a loss at all by the person involved. But where a certain level of engagement has been reached and some agreed progress has been made, there may be complex and mixed emotions about ending. Strategies for managing such endings include:

- discussing endings right from the start, so that people are prepared
- paying careful attention to the emotions that endings can raise in everyone involved (supervision may be an important tool here)
- phasing the ending of any support, so that confidence can be gained.

Learning this skill will help you to meet the following National Occupational Standards:

Key Role 2: Unit 5.
Key Role 5: Unit 14.

Skills for Evaluation

Evaluation may not be immediately recognised as a social work skill. When people think of evaluations of service delivery, they usually think of one-off large-scale exercises, often planned and carried out by an independent evaluator. Such evaluations can have important consequences for an agency's strategic planning. Does the service do what it claims? Is it cost effective? Could the money be better spent elsewhere?

This is not really the kind of evaluation that we will consider here, although there are common features. Evaluations considered in this chapter are much more routine, less formalised and much closer to the kind of thinking that goes on during and at the end of individual pieces of work. So social workers might well ask themselves to what extent their intervention was successful, what made the difference, whether they were happy with their own performance, whether there were things that they could have done better, and whether there were external constraints that limited their effectiveness.

How do social workers evaluate their own work?

There is some evidence that social workers make precisely this distinction between two different kinds of evaluation. In a study of fifteen recently qualified social workers, practice teachers and experienced practitioners in England and Wales, Shaw (1996) shows how they talk about 'proper' evaluation, defining it as follows:

- part of a performance culture
- experienced as scrutiny from above
- formal, planned and occasional, not ongoing
- relatively time-consuming
- measured quantitatively, not qualitatively
- responding to expectations created from above and from outside of direct practice
- focusing on service-level concerns, not on direct practice.

Experiences of this kind of evaluation were mostly negative. There was strong scepticism about the kinds of measurements that were used and about the relevance of the findings. Workers were concerned that outcomes were more likely to be a prelude to the latest disruptive reorganisation than to any real increase in resources.

This is contrasted with social workers' own kind of 'informal system of measurement to see whether I'm doing what I see as being *a good job*' (Shaw, 1996: 38). Such self-evaluation has the following features. It is:

- about quality and worth, not about quantity
- personal, informal, private and subjective

- not part of core practice skills but an add-on
- in need of a long-term perspective
- drawing on complex evidence that is not easy to interpret
- assuming that progress is typically by slow, incremental steps
- connected with personal commitments and values
- sometimes drawing on 'proper' evaluation methods.

Note that the social workers in this study understood such self-evaluation as being outside of the normal processes of casework. It is a personal add-on that is not talked about, even informally, in the office. It is a way of making sense of one's individual commitment to the job, of asking whether what one did in any particular case was right and whether it actually made any difference. It is quite different from the formal topics that might be discussed in supervision. This mode seems to be particularly relevant in statutory contexts, where the rewards of a job well done may be difficult to find and outcomes may be of the 'least bad' variety. Two questions follow from this. First, how do social workers go about their task? Second, why is this kind of evaluation not seen as a more formal part of the work?

Shaw's (1996) research suggests that social workers commonly have a broad strategy for successful casework, against which they measure things. This includes having an implicit 'game plan' that is somewhat different from any formal goals and methods for the intervention, such as might be recorded in a written case plan. An important element of the 'game plan' is to stay in control of the case rather than be dragged along by events. Clear and constructive goals are an important help here, as well as an accurate understanding of the legal and procedural framework – the 'rules of the game'. It is also necessary to have a detailed understanding of the individuals involved, so as to employ timely interventions and stay 'ahead of the game'. However, social workers also acknowledged the significance of 'sheer luck'. Some cases lead to a real 'connection' with the individual involved and to real change, whilst others just 'blow up' and become very difficult. The idea of 'luck' reflected the belief that the factors influencing these outcomes were often outside of the social worker's control.

When it comes to social workers assessing the quality of their own work, Shaw's (1996) study shows that another group of questions is important:

- Are there emotional rewards or penalties?
- Did the intervention lead to steady, incremental change?
- Was the problem previously 'stuck' or 'moving'?

- Did fellow professionals suggest that the work was of good quality?
- Has the process harmed the person involved?
- Did the person involved give any positive feedback?

It appears that social workers use the evidence of their own feelings as an important measure of the success of the work. Work that is going well becomes 'a real pleasure'. There is 'a buzz'. On the other hand, when things are going badly there is a sense of frustration. But are these feelings really a good guide to the quality of the work? Psychodynamic approaches to therapy would certainly suggest that workers' emotional responses are an important source of evidence about the progress of the work itself. This argument was presented more fully in Chapter 3, in the context of using supervision to help with the analysis. The argument is that the business of interpreting these feelings is complex, and this is why supervision is important.

Feelings are not everything, and evidence of change in the situation was also important. Social workers looked for evidence of change in the people they worked with: change in behaviour and change in attitude. However, they were acutely aware of the difficulty of telling whether such change was a result of their intervention or whether it would have happened anyway. They were also wary of setting, or claiming to have achieved, ambitious goals. They seemed more than satisfied with evidence of small changes, particularly when the situation had previously been stuck.

What about the views of service users?

As we have seen in the list above, one of the ways in which social workers evaluate the quality of their own work is by looking out for examples of feedback from the people involved. However, particularly in statutory contexts, there are real difficulties in obtaining and making sense of such feedback.

One fundamental question is the degree to which we should expect those involved to be satisfied with the actions of social workers. If social work is imposed on someone, then we might well expect that person to resist and, if asked, to provide negative feedback. So perhaps good social workers are those who attract negative comments from those they work with? Some social workers certainly seem to regard formal complaints as a badge of honour. But, as we have seen, this kind of antagonistic relationship is not the full picture of social work in statutory contexts. Most is carried out in more ambiguous relationships, which contain some elements of partnership and some meaningful engagement. This is then reflected in a complex feedback.

Consider case example 8.1 on page 161. Darren has been subject to a referral order that has now ended without him reoffending. Darren was angry about the prosecution; he was never happy about his lack of choice in accepting the intervention. However, his experience of the support services was positive and the final outcome was the one that he had been working for: an end to the order. Overall, his feeling afterwards was that he should have been able to get some help in dealing with his anger without the prosecution.

In this example there is only partial agreement in the evaluation of the work. In the end there is no way of telling whether Darren's claim is true and whether the changes could have been achieved without the referral order. However, the social worker's position is that the requirements of justice and the desire to reduce the risk of reoffending meant that order was both necessary and justified. The differences in evaluation are related to differences in power and legal responsibility.

This should come as no surprise. But relative differences in power can influence feedback from service users in a number of important ways. First, it is possible that it makes no sense at all to be asked to make judgements about the quality of a service that you have not asked for and don't have control over. Resigned acceptance might be a more realistic stance. Second, people may not be in a position to complain, for fear of negative consequences. Finally, there is evidence to show that customer satisfaction in various contexts away from social work is heavily influenced by what people expect, rather than by the level of service per se. That is to say, an average meal served in a five-star restaurant is likely to receive a lower satisfaction rating than the same meal served in a local snack bar. In statutory contexts, people who expect heavy-handed interventions may be less upset if they experience them than those who expect sensitivity.

Knowledge about the roles and responsibilities of social workers is also likely to be influential here. Arguably, someone who understands and, crucially, accepts statutory social work roles will evaluate the work differently from someone who does not. This suggests that the quality of the engagement phase, during which social workers explain their role and statutory duties, may ultimately affect the person's overall evaluation of the work.

Whilst feedback from service users must be a part of the evaluation, it is difficult to know how best to obtain and to interpret it in individual cases. However, some basic principles are clear. There is a need to talk to service users about how their voice can be heard. This should include discussion about safeguards in situations where service users may be concerned about potential negative consequences of criticism. There is a need to take action as a result of feedback, whilst one remains open about any limitations arising from the statutory context.

Evaluating social work in statutory contexts

There is no doubt that evaluation is growing in importance in social work and that it links to broad policy aims of increasing effectiveness and efficiency. However, evaluation is also significant at the level of individual cases and is an ongoing part of social workers' attempts to make sense of the complexity of what they do. At this level there is evidence that social workers draw on their own subjective experience of the work and on that of service users when assessing its quality, and that they look for evidence of slow, incremental change. This could be done more rigorously and formally, for instance in supervision or in case recording.

Walker and Beckett (2003) suggest that it is helpful to distinguish between two broad types of evidence: the 'subjective' experiences of social workers and service users and the 'objective' evaluation of whether specific goals were achieved. Using this distinction to think again about Darren – case example 8.1 on page 161 – we can see that, although this is a helpful framework, it does not solve all the problems. In this case, the subjective experiences of those involved are clear enough, but fundamental differences in their feelings about the referral order are not easy to resolve. This difference is also significant in the objective evaluation of whether the goals were achieved. The social worker's goal of reducing reoffending was rather different from Darren's objective of getting to the end of the order with the minimum contact with his social worker. We need to be clear about whose specific goals we are talking about.

Skill summary: Evaluating work

This can be seen as an under-developed area of social work practice. There is evidence to suggest that social workers routinely ask themselves about the successes and failures of their work and about its quality and usefulness. However, much of this evaluation may be personal and informal, linked to social workers' own internal values and reasons for doing the job. There is a case for trying to develop this kind of evaluation and for making it more rigorous and formal. Strategies for skilled practice in evaluation include:

- setting and reviewing specific goals
- being able to draw on qualitative and quantitative methods of evaluation
- understanding the significance of workers' feelings as a guide to success
- taking into account the differing aims and experiences of service users.

Learning this skill will help you to meet the following National Occupational Standards:

Key Role 5: Unit 14.
Key Role 6: Units 18, 19, 20 and 21.

Skills for Reflective Practice

This particular set of skills builds on some of the concepts that were developed in the previous section on evaluation. Here we drew a distinction between 'proper' evaluation, which might be undertaken typically by an independent evaluator as a one-off event, and social workers' own, personal evaluations of individual pieces of work. This distinction is broadly in line with the distinction that might be made between evidence-based practice and reflective practice. The following sections consider what is meant by both phrases. Finally, we will consider the concept of 'critical reflection' and its significance in statutory contexts. Note that we have moved away from considering what happens just at the end of a piece of work, to a form of practice that has the potential to run right through all stages of the work.

Evidence-based practice

This is practice based on the idea that decision-making should be justified by sound evidence, derived from rigorous research. This applies equally at all levels of the organisation, from planning and resource allocation right down to individual cases. So money should not be spent, for example, on setting up groups to support children who have witnessed domestic violence unless it can be shown that such groups work. And social workers should draw on evidence, for example about the effects of drugs on parenting when they argue that this is likely to be a factor in a particular case. The movement towards evidence-based practice is, in part, a reaction to the criticism that welfare agencies have relied too much on arbitrary custom and practice (we've always done it this way) and have not changed in response to changed circumstances. This movement is part of the wider agenda of the modernisation of local government, which was discussed in Chapter 1.

Case example 8.3a

George is a social worker in a local authority fostering and adoption team in England. He has recently carried out an annual review of foster carers Helen and Alan Smith. Such reviews are a statutory requirement under s.29 of the Fostering Services Regulations (Department of Health, 2002a). Helen and Alan are in their early fifties, white and British, and have grown-up children who have left home. They were first approved two years ago and they are currently approved to take up to five children of any age. Under the terms of s.29, the purpose of such a review is to determine 'whether the person continues to be suitable as to act as a foster parent and his household continues to be suitable' and whether 'the terms of his approval continue to be appropriate'. A formal report will be written and taken to a fostering panel meeting for approval.

During the process of carrying out the review, George has spoken to Helen and Alan themselves. He has also seen the older children and the young people who have been placed with Helen and Alan during the year and has spoken to their social workers. Here is a summary of those discussions:

- Helen and Alan described it as a difficult year. They felt that the teenagers who were placed with them have been particularly challenging to manage. Marcus, a young man aged 15 and black, had been missing overnight on several occasions and was eventually arrested for a serious offence, which led to a placement with remand foster carers. Helen and Alan felt that this was an admission by the local authority that he should not have been placed with them in the first place. They said that they were not sad to see him go. Other placements included three white girls aged 9, 12 and 14, who were sisters. Helen and Alan said that it had been difficult to control the large network of friends and boyfriends who kept visiting and whom the girls wanted to spend time with. They were happier caring for two younger white children: Ben, aged 3, and Amy, aged 4.

- The young people welcomed some aspects of the foster placement. They were particularly appreciative of the food. But there were also a number of complaints. Marcus felt that the rules were ridiculously strict for him as a 15-year-old. This was why he had spent so much time out of the home. The three sisters complained about having to share a room, about the physically cramped conditions in the small house, and about the strict rules.
- The social workers also had reservations about the placements. Marcus' social worker felt that there had been a lack of the necessary flexibility in setting boundaries for him. She also felt that Helen and Alan simply hadn't liked Marcus and that this had been clear to him throughout. The social worker for the teenage sisters was concerned that Helen and Alan did not seem to have understood the impact which physical and sexual abuse had had on the girls before they were placed and, in particular, that Helen and Andrew had found it difficult to deal with the girls' anger and with aspects of their sexual behaviour. The social workers for the younger children, Ben and Amy, felt that the standard of physical care was fine, but that there had been some lack of emotional warmth.

Following these enquiries, George prepared a written review report. His recommendations were as follows:

- that Helen and Andrew's approval should be reduced from five children to three
- that they should agree to attend some further training in relation to children's emotional needs, behaviour management and the impact of abuse.

Exercise 8.1

Referring to the information given in case example 8.3a, what would you identify as the evidence base that underlies George's concerns about the placement and his recommendations about further training?

In relation to understanding children's emotional needs we might draw on insights from attachment theory. This theory emphasises the importance of emotional warmth for children's development (see, for example, Holmes, 1993).

In relation to managing the behaviour of teenagers we might refer to recent research by Farmer and colleagues (2004). This research shows how successful foster carers tend to reverse the more normal process of control and discipline in families. Whereas it may be usual to establish firm controls early on and then gradually to relax them as young people mature and become more independent, successful foster carers tend to be fairly relaxed about boundaries at first and then, as time goes on, tighten them to some degree within the normal range. This reflects the fact that many young people entering foster placement have not experienced strong controls previously and may react badly to their sudden imposition. However, control is not abandoned but rather introduced steadily, as a working relationship is built up. The same research shows that successful foster carers are those who actually like the young people whom they look after and are able to communicate this feeling.

In relation to the impact of abuse on children, the evidence base is diverse and substantial. Some significant studies include:

- Gibbons and colleagues (1995) on the impact of physical abuse
- Gardner (2008) on responding to emotional abuse and neglect
- Finkelhor and Browne (1986) on the impact of sexual abuse
- Batty (1991) on making placements work for sexually abused children.

(This brief discussion of fostering has been introduced as a way of illustrating some wider points about evidence-based practice. The research listed above represents some of the evidence that might be relevant to George's work. It certainly does not constitute a thorough or comprehensive review of the field.)

So what are the strengths and limitations of using an evidence-based approach? The overwhelming strength is that it seems entirely rational and sensible to base interventions on what is known, in this case about the needs of children who are looked after and about the way they can be met. If we want to help people, then why would we ignore evidence about the best ways to do it? However, the problem is that, as Shaw points out, too much is assumed. 'What do we mean by "evidence"? What do we mean by "practice"? How is one "based" on the other?' (Shaw, 1999: 3).

First there is the question of what counts as evidence. There are debates and disagreements about this within the field. At its narrowest, there are those who believe that evidence should come from studies which provide objective measurements, preferably from quantitative studies with experimental or quasi-experimental designs. The danger here is that much of what might count as knowledge in social work could be excluded. Others will accept additional forms of evidence, for example from qualitative research, theoretical writing and practice wisdom. At the heart of the debate are questions about the status of scientific knowledge itself. Those who study the sociology of scientific knowledge (for example Latour, 1999) have shown the processes by which scientific knowledge is made, rather than revealed. The argument is that, although scientists present their work in a tidy and authoritative style, the reality is that scientific practice is rather more messy and disjointed. More importantly, such messiness includes personal and social influences on the research process that are not reported in formal findings. Those who seek to extend our understanding of what counts as evidence in social work will argue that scientific knowledge has much more in common with practice wisdom than is ever acknowledged within scientific writing, and that sources of evidence of a wide variety are relevant.

The second question is about how evidence can be used in practice. This is a more difficult and complex process than it might at first appear. Take the fostering review that was referred to above. The research studies that were listed may be relevant, but what do they say about this particular case? They give a rationale for providing emotional warmth to children in placement and a way of understanding the behaviour of abused children. But what should the social worker George do as a result? One of the key questions was whether the parenting being provided by Helen and Alan was actually good enough to warrant their re-approval at all. This evidence base does not offer a straightforward measurement scale with a clear cut-off point; it supplies instead the context for making an informed, professional judgement. Social work practice should draw on the best available evidence about what works. But we should think critically about the kind of evidence that we are prepared to draw upon, and we should be aware that making use of that evidence in individual cases remains a skilled professional task.

Reflective practice

Case example 8.3b

What follows is an account of what happened when George was called to discuss his report with Helen and Alan a few days before the formal meeting of the fostering panel. First, George clarified the procedural basis of the review and framed it as an opportunity for learning and for growth. He gave Helen and Andrew time to read the report and then he invited their comments.

Alan said that he didn't understand what the problem was. They had had some difficult young people to care for and had done so to the best of their ability. 15-year old Marcus, in particular, had been beyond their control and, in their view, inappropriately placed. Alan said he thought that anyone would have struggled.

George acknowledged that looking after Marcus had been challenging. He also acknowledged that having their parenting scrutinised in this kind of detail must be difficult for the two of them, particularly when Helen and Alan were being asked to do such a difficult job. The review was therefore a chance to work out how to develop their skills in order to progress further.

Helen said she felt that working with the three sisters had been hard. She had felt unsure of what to say to them and of how to react to some of their behaviour. For example, the 9-year-old was always tearing things up and destroying her toys. Helen could not understand this and had ended up keeping the toys in the cupboard, out of harm's way. She also said that the child's nightmares had been difficult to handle, because she had not felt able to comfort the child in the way she would have comforted her own children.

George reminded them of some of the initial training they had received, which dealt with managing the behaviour of abused children. Again, he acknowledged the difficulty of the task and the need to develop Helen's and Alan's understanding of how to manage the behaviour of such children whilst also meeting their emotional needs. The discussion continued for about an hour and, at the end of that time, Helen and Alan were actively signed up for attending further training and a foster carer support group.

Reflective practice means drawing not just on the relevant evidence base from formal research, but on a much wider range of thinking and insights into the particular circumstances of the situation. In this case example, George understands that his report is more than just a technical or rational application of the evidence base to one particular case. The report is also likely to be seen as criticism of Helen's and Alan's parenting, or even as a threat (further training or we may end your approval). So, when talking with Helen and Alan, George acknowledges the difficulties that some of the young people posed, thus making the difficulties seem more understandable, and he reframes the problem as a chance to develop more skills.

Reflective practice is mostly associated with the work of Donald Schön (1995). Schön argues that, when working with people, there is such variety and complexity that there cannot be a straightforward technical solution to problems. Professionals working with people need to acknowledge the uniqueness of the individuals involved. They must understand the relevance of the inter-subjective dynamics (in our example, this includes the experience of being criticised or threatened). They need to do it both during their work and afterwards. This provides the basis for the distinction between reflection in action (that is, reflection at the time of acting) and reflection on action (afterwards). Awareness of the processes and dynamics that were going on in the meeting enabled George to make them explicit and to acknowledge how uncomfortable it was for Helen and Alan to have their parenting scrutinised in detail. Whilst this did not completely solve the problem, it offered both a way around the question of blame and a basis on which the three of them could talk about why skills development was necessary.

Since Schön's work was originally published, the idea of reflective practice has been developed further by others (Knott, 2007). Ruch (2007) identifies four different types of reflective practice: technical reflection, practical reflection, process reflection and critical reflection. Three of these are outlined briefly below, while the fourth, critical reflection, is the topic of the next section.

- *Technical reflection* has a rather precise focus on problem solving. It tends to concentrate on the question of how the formal evidence base that we considered earlier is used in practice.

- *Practical reflection* adds an awareness of the significance of inter-subjectivity, which we have already examined. In addition, it includes an awareness of personal and professional assumptions that may be influencing practice. For example George may be aware that he feels strongly about the need for children to express difficult feelings. He realises that this could make it difficult for him to understand the practical difficulties associated with managing children who want to break toys. His reflective awareness of the difference between himself and Helen on this topic means that he avoids appearing to be dismissive of her concerns.

- *Process reflection* emphasises the dynamics of the relationships between the people involved. It uses psychodynamic insights to understand some of the complex processes of mirroring and transference and to help workers to deal with the unavoidable impact of the emotional content of the work (see Chapter 3).

Critical reflection

Critical reflection can be thought of as consisting of each of the previous types of reflection, but with an additional feature. As Fook (2002) puts it:

> Being reflective and being critically reflective share important similarities. Both involve a recognition of how we, as knowers, participate in creating and generating the knowledge we use, and an appreciation of how knowledge is therefore contingent upon the holistic context in which it is created. A reflective stance points up the many and diverse perspectives which can be taken on knowledge itself, and the shaping of that knowledge. The important difference is that critical reflection places emphasis and importance on understanding [. . .] how a reflective stance uncovers power relations, and how structures of domination are created and maintained. (Fook, 2002: 41)

It is this distinctive focus on power relations that distinguishes critical reflection from other forms of reflection. Because of this focus, it is easy to see that critical reflection fits well with transformational views of social work and with emancipatory values (see Chapter 2). What could this mean in practice? Consider exercise 8.2.

Exercise 8.2

Referring again to the information given in case example 8.3, what do you think are the key power relationships that are having an impact on George's work with Helen and Alan?

There are two broad categories of power relationships. First there are the power relationships between adults and children in general terms. The idea of children's rights is important to George. He has made sure that the views of the children and young people have informed the conclusions of his review. But he is concerned that potentially oppressive stereotypes about out-of-control teenagers, and particularly about black teenagers, may have had an impact on how Marcus was treated, both within the placement and more generally.

Second, there are the power relationships between George as a local authority social worker and Helen and Alan as foster carers. Whilst foster carers are not usually employees, nonetheless the local authority, through the fostering panel, retains the ability to hire and fire and, with it, the responsibility to maintain standards of care. This would seem to put George in a relatively powerful position. However, set against this is the fact that the local authority is highly dependent on the goodwill and the skills of its foster carers in order to provide care for looked-after children. Foster carers may resign if they feel that the demands on them are unreasonable. There is interplay of power rather than a binary division between the powerful and the powerless.

Reflective practice in statutory contexts

In Chapter 2 we considered some difficulties in applying the principles of empowerment and partnership – central tenets of anti-oppressive practice – in statutory contexts. It may be that the legitimate aim of a statutory intervention is to control an individual's abusive behaviour and that this is fundamentally at odds with empowerment and partnership. However, that discussion pointed to the fluidity and complexity of power relations between workers and service users, and sometimes between family members. It questioned the significance of binary distinctions, particularly between care and control, and pointed to the productive use of power.

The case example we have been discussing illustrates similar tensions in a particular statutory context, which concerns the continuing approval of Helen and Alan as foster carers. As we have seen, critical reflection means uncovering power relations and taking them into account. But some of these dynamics of power are an instrumental part of the statutory context. For example, the responsibility for maintaining standards of care and the associated power to terminate foster carers' approval is fundamental to George's statutory role. It does not make any sense to suggest that he should give up this power as a way of empowering Helen and Alan. Critical reflection in statutory contexts means understanding power relations and asking critical questions about their legitimacy.

Skill summary: Practising reflectively

Reflective practice is about the links between thinking and doing. It is committed to using the best possible evidence about what works and why. But at the same time it extends our ideas about what constitutes knowledge, to make them include informal sources such as practice wisdom. An important feature of reflective practice is the fact that workers are able to position themselves, their assumptions, values and emotions in relation to the task and, in critical reflection, to understand the relevance of power relations. Strategies for reflective practice include:

- finding the relevant evidence base
- applying it to a particular context
- taking an holistic view of the situation
- understanding the inter-subjective dynamics, including the emotional impact
- uncovering power relations
- considering the productive exercise of power in the particular statutory setting.

Learning this skill will help you to meet the following National Occupational Standards:

Key Role 2: Unit 6.
Key Role 6: Unit 19 and Unit 20.

Conclusion

Social work in statutory contexts starts with the legal duties of the social worker's employing agency. So, when one is making decisions about ending an intervention and evaluating the outcomes, the first question must be about the degree to which those duties have been fulfilled. But this is not to argue that other considerations are irrelevant. For example, the views of those affected by the intervention are very significant. But, in line with the approach taken throughout this book, those views must be considered in the light of the legal duties that are driving the intervention.

This does not mean that social workers undertaking statutory interventions will always be in opposition to those they are working with. As we have seen, some of those affected may welcome some or all of the interventions, and skilled practice seeks to maximise opportunities to give choice and control and to work in partnership when this helps to fulfil the legal duty. We have seen this principle at work throughout the book, as we have considered the nature of skilled practice in relation to the various stages of work. Underlying this approach is the need for critical reflection on the nature of the power relationships involved. We need to keep under constant review questions about the aims and legitimacy of particular interventions, and about how the principles of anti-oppressive practice fit with the aims of the work.

Whilst it seems that formal evaluation of social work interventions is not well developed, nonetheless there is evidence that individual social workers find it important to reflect on completed work. In the light of the current pressures on social workers in statutory settings – pressures that were identified in the Introduction and in Chapter 1 – it is more important than ever that individuals are supported in their commitment to the job. Supervisors have an important role in helping social workers with their own assessment of whether or not what they did in any particular case was right and actually made any difference.

Further Reading

Holmes, J. (1993) *John Bowlby and Attachment Theory*. London: Routledge. An introduction to attachment theory and the concept of 'loss'.

Knott, C. (2007) *Reflective Practice in Social Work*. Exeter: Learning Matters. A useful introduction to the concept of reflective practice written for social workers in training.

Shaw, I. (1996) *Evaluating in Practice*. Aldershot: Arena. Describes a strategy for reflective evaluating in social work practice that draws on qualitative methods.

Appendix: National Occupational Standards for Social Work

This is a shortened version of the National Occupational Standards for Social Work, showing the Key Roles and Units referred to throughout the book. Full details are available on the Skills for Care website.

www.skillsforcare.org.uk/developing_skills/National_Occupational_Standards/social_work.aspx

Key Role 1: **Prepare for, and work with, individuals, families, carers, groups and communities to assess their needs and circumstances**

Unit 1   Prepare for social work contact and involvement

Unit 2   Work with individuals, families, carers, groups and communities to help them make informed decisions

Unit 3   Assess needs and options to recommend a course of action

Key Role 2: **Plan, carry out, review and evaluate social work practice, with individuals, families, carers, groups, communities and other professionals**

Unit 4   Respond to crisis situations

Unit 5   Interact with individuals, families, carers, groups and communities to achieve change and development and to improve life opportunities

Unit 6	Prepare, produce, implement and evaluate plans with individuals, families, carers, groups, communities and professional colleagues
Unit 7	Support the development of networks to meet assessed needs and planned outcomes
Unit 8	Work with groups to promote individual growth, development and independence
Unit 9	Address behaviour which presents a risk to individuals, families, carers, groups and communities
Key Role 3:	**Support individuals to represent their needs, views and circumstances**
Unit 10	Advocate with, and on behalf of, individuals, families, carers, groups and communities
Unit 11	Prepare for, and participate in, decision-making forums
Key Role 4:	**Manage risk to individuals, families, carers, groups, communities, self and colleagues**
Unit 12	Assess and manage risks to individuals, families, carers, groups and communities
Unit 13	Assess, minimise and manage risk to self and colleagues
Key Role 5:	**Manage and be accountable for, with supervision and support, your own social work practice within your organisation**
Unit 14	Manage and be accountable for your own work
Unit 15	Contribute to the management of resources and services
Unit 16	Manage, present and share records and reports
Unit 17	Work within multi-disciplinary and multi-organisational teams, networks and systems
Key Role 6:	**Demonstrate professional competence in social work practice**
Unit 18	Research, analyse, evaluate and use current knowledge of best social work practice

Unit 19   Work within agreed standards of social work practice and ensure own professional development

Unit 20   Manage complex ethical issues, dilemmas and conflicts

Unit 21   Contribute to the promotion of best social work practice

References

Adams, R. (2003) *Social Work and Empowerment*, 3rd edn. Basingstoke: Palgrave Macmillan.

Adams, R., Dominelli, L. and Payne, M. (eds) (2002) *Critical Practice in Social Work*. Basingstoke: Palgrave Macmillan.

Amphlett, S. (1998) 'The experience of a watchdog', in G. Hunt (ed.), *Whistleblowing in the Social Services*, pp. 65–93. London: Routledge.

Andrew, J. (2008) *Baby P Case 'May Scare Staff Off'*. Available at: http://news.bbc.co.uk/1/hi/uk/7775857.stm (accessed 3 April 2009).

Banks, S. (2002) 'Professional values and accountabilities', in R. Adams, L. Dominelli and M. Payne (eds), *Critical Practice in Social Work*, pp. 28–37. Basingstoke: Palgrave Macmillan.

Banks, S. (2004) *Ethics, Accountability and the Social Professions*. Basingstoke: Palgrave Macmillan.

Banks, S. (2006) *Ethics and Values in Social Work*, 3rd edn. Basingstoke: Palgrave Macmillan.

Bannister, A. and Huntingdon, A. (2002) *Communicating with Children and Adolescents*. London: Jessica Kingsley Publishers.

BASW (2002) *The Code of Ethics for Social Work*. Birmingham: BASW.

Batty, D. (1991) *Sexually Abused Children: Making Their Placements Work*. London: British Agencies for Adoption and Fostering.

Beckett, C. (2007) *Child Protection: An Introduction*, 2nd edn. London: Sage.

Beckett, C. and Maynard, A. (2005) *Values and Ethics in Social Work*. London: Sage.

Beckett, C., McKeigue, B. and Taylor, H. (2007) 'Coming to conclusions: Social workers' perceptions of the decision-making process in care proceedings', *Child and Family Social Work*, 12(1): 54–63.

Bell, M. (1996) 'An account of the experiences of 51 families involved in an initial child protection conference', *Child and Family Social Work*, 1(1): 43–55.

Bell, M. (1999) *Child Protection: Families and the Conference Process.* Aldershot: Ashgate.

Biestek, F. (1961) *The Casework Relationship.* London: Allen and Unwin.

Blair, T. (1998) *The Third Way: New Politics for the New Century.* London: The Fabian Society.

Bowlby, J. (1973) *Separation, Anxiety and Anger.* London: Hogarth Press.

Braithwaite, R. (2001) *Managing Aggression.* London: Routledge.

Brandon, M., Schofield, G. and Trinder, L. (1998) *Social Work with Children.* Basingstoke: Macmillan.

Braye, S. and Preston-Shoot, M. (1997) *Practising Social Work Law*, 2nd edn. Basingstoke: Macmillan.

Brayne, H. and Carr, H. (2008) *Law for Social Workers*, 10th edn. Oxford: Oxford University Press.

Brown, H., Fry, E. and Howard, J. (2005) *Support Care: How Family Placements Can Keep Children and Families Together.* Lyme Regis: Russell House Publishing.

Buckley, B. (2003) *Children's Communication Skills: From Birth to Five Years.* London: Routledge.

Burke, B. and Harrison, P. (2002) 'Anti-oppressive practice', in R. Adams, L. Dominelli and M. Payne (eds), *Social Work: Themes, Issues and Critical Debates*, pp. 227–36. Basingstoke: Palgrave Macmillan.

Butterworth, R. (2004) 'Managing violence', in T. Ryan and J. Pritchard (eds), *Good Practice in Adult Mental Health*, pp. 311–32. London: Routledge.

Calder, M. (2001) *Mothers of Sexually Abused Children: A Framework for Understanding and Support.* Lyme Regis: Russell House Publishing.

Calder, M. (2003) 'The Assessment Framework: A critique and reformulation', in C. Calder and S. Hackett (eds), *Assessment in Child Care: Using and Developing Frameworks for Practice*, pp. 3–60. Lyme Regis: Russell House Publishing.

Calder, M. (2008) 'A framework for working with resistance, motivation and change', in M. Calder (ed.), *The Carrot or the Stick? Towards Effective Practice with Involuntary Clients in Safeguarding Children Work*, pp. 120–40. Lyme Regis: Russell House Publishing.

Calder, M. (ed.) (2008) *The Carrot or the Stick? Towards Effective Practice with Involuntary Clients in Safeguarding Children Work*, Lyme Regis: Russell House Publishing.

CCETSW (1989) *Requirements and Regulations for the Diploma in Social Work.* London: CCETSW.

Clarke, J., Gewirtz, S. and McLaughlin, E. (eds) (2000) *New Managerialism, New Welfare?* London: Sage.

Cleaver, H. and Walker, S. (2004) *Assessing Children's Needs and Circumstances: The Impact of the Assessment Framework.* London: Jessica Kingsley Publishers.

Collingridge, M., Miller, S. and Bowles, W. (2001) 'Privacy and confidentiality in social work', *Australian Social Work*, 54(2): 3–13.

Cooper, P. (2006) *Reporting to Court under the Children Act: A Handbook for Social Services*, 2nd edn. London: TSO.

Corby, B. (1996) 'Risk assessment in child protection work', in H. Kemshall and J. Pritchard (eds), *Good Practice in Risk Assessment and Risk Management*, pp. 13–30. London: Jessica Kingsley Publishers.

Corby, B., Millar, M. and Young, L. (1996) 'Parental participation in child protection work: Rethinking the rhetoric', *British Journal of Social Work*, 26: 475–92.

Corden, J. and Somerton, J. (2004) 'The trans-theoretical model of change: A reliable blueprint for assessment in work with children and families?', *British Journal of Social Work*, 34: 1025–44.

Corrigan, P. and Leonard, P. (1978) *Social Work Practice under Capitalism: A Marxist Approach*. London: Macmillan.

Coulshed, V. and Orme, J. (2006) *Social Work Practice: An Introduction*, 4th edn. Basingstoke: Palgrave Macmillan.

Cree, V. (2002) 'The changing nature of social work', in R. Adams, L. Dominelli and M. Payne (eds), *Social Work: Themes, Issues and Critical Debates*, 2nd edn, pp. 20–9. Basingstoke: Palgrave Macmillan.

Cross, M. (2004) *Children with Emotional and Behavioural Difficulties and Communication Problems: There Is Always a Reason*. London: Jessica Kingsley Publishers.

Currer, C. (2007) *Loss and Social Work*. Exeter: Learning Matters.

Dalrymple, J. and Burke, B. (2006) *Anti-Oppressive Practice: Social Care and the Law*, 2nd edn. Buckingham: Open University Press.

Davies, L. (2008) 'Reclaiming the language of child protection', in M. Calder (ed.), *Contemporary Risk Assessment in Safeguarding Children*, pp. 25–39. Lyme Regis: Russell House Publishing.

Davies, M. (1994) *The Essential Social Worker*, 3rd edn. Aldershot: Arena.

Davis, L. (2007) *See You in Court: A Social Worker's Guide to Presenting Evidence in Care Proceedings*. London: Jessica Kingsley Publishers.

De Jong, P. and Berg, I. (2001) 'Co-constructing cooperation with mandated clients', *Social Work*, 46(4): 361–74.

Department for Children, Schools and Families (2005) *Every Child Matters*. Available at: http://www.everychildmatters.gov.uk/aims/childrenstrusts/ (accessed 19 November 2007).

Department for Children, Schools and Families (2008) *The Children Act 1989: Guidance and Regulations*, Vol. 1: *Court Orders*. London: TSO.

Department for Children, Schools and Families (2009) *Ed Balls and Alan Johnson Announce Members and Remit of Social Work Taskforce*. Available at: http://www.dcsf.gov.uk/pns/DisplayPN.cgi?pn_id=2009_0017 (accessed 3 April 2009).

Department of Health (1995a) *Child Protection: Messages From Research*. London: HMSO.

Department of Health (1995b) *The Challenge of Partnership in Child Protection: Practice Guide*. London: HMSO.

Department of Health (1998) *Modernising Social Services: Promoting Independence, Improving Protection, Raising Standards*. Cm 4169. London: HMSO.

Department of Health (1999) *Care Plans and Care Proceedings under the Children Act 1989. Local Authority Circular (LAC (99) 29)*. London: Department of Health.

Department of Health (2000a) *A Quality Strategy For Social Care*. London: Department of Health.

Department of Health (2000b) *Framework for the Assessment of Children in Need and Their Families*. London: The Stationery Office.

Department of Health (2002a) *Fostering Services Regulations*. London: The Stationery Office.

Department of Health (2002b) *LAC (2002)13: Fair Access to Care Services: Guidance on Eligibility Criteria for Adult Social Care*. Available at: http://www.dh.gov.uk/en/Publicationsandstatistics/Lettersandcirculars/Local-AuthorityCirculars/AllLocalAuthority/DH_4004734 (accessed 1 April 2008).

Department of Health (2002c) *Requirements for Social Work Training*. London: HMSO.

Department of Health (2002d) *Single Assessment Process*. Available at: http://www.dh.gov.uk/en/SocialCare/Chargingandassessment/Single AssessmentProcess/DH_079509#_1 (accessed 9 April 2008).

Department of Health (2007) *What Is Social Work: The Role*. Available at: http://www.socialworkandcare.co.uk/socialwork/what/index.asp (accessed 24 April 2007).

Department of Health (2008) *Code of Practice: Mental Health Act 1983*. London: TSO.

Department of Health, NSPCC and Chailey Heritage (1997) *Turning Points: A Resource Pack for Communicating with Children*. London: NSPCC.

Dickens, J. (2005) 'Being "the epitome of reason": The challenges for lawyers and social workers in child care proceedings', *International Journal of Law, Policy and the Family*, 19(1): 73–101.

Dickens, J. (2006) 'Care, control and change in child care proceedings: Dilemmas for social workers, managers and lawyers', *Child and Family Social Work*, 11(1): 23–32.

DiClemente, C. (1991) 'Motivational interviewing and the stages of change', in W. Miller and S. Rollnick (eds), *Motivational Interviewing: Preparing People to Change Addictive Behaviour*, pp. 191–202. London: Guilford Press.

Dominelli, L. (1997) *Sociology for Social Work*. Basingstoke: Macmillan.

Dominelli, L. (2002) *Feminist Social Work: Theory and Practice*. Basingstoke: Palgrave Macmillan.

Dominelli, L. (2004) *Social Work: Theory and Practice for a Changing Profession*. Cambridge: Polity Press.

Drakeford, M. (2000) *Privatisation and Social Policy*. Harlow: Longman.

Egan, G. (2006) *The Skilled Helper: A Problem-Management and Opportunity Development Approach to Helping*, 3rd edn. London: Wadsworth.

Exworthy, M. and Halford, S. (1999) 'Professionals and managers in a changing public sector: Conflict, compromise and collaboration?', in M. Exworthy and S. Halford (eds), *Professionals and the New Managerialism in the Public Sector*, pp. 1–17. Buckingham: Open University Press.

Farmer, E., Moyers, S. and Lipscombe, J. (2004) *Fostering Adolescents*. London: Jessica Kingsley Publishers.

Featherstone, B. and Fawcett, B. (1994) 'Feminism and child abuse: Opening up some possibilities?', *Critical Social Policy*, 14(3): 61–80.

Ferguson, H. (2004) *Protecting Children in Time: Child Abuse, Child Protection and the Consequences of Modernity*. Basingstoke: Palgrave Macmillan.

Ferguson, H. (2008) *Social Workers Are Better Now at Child Protection*. Available at: http://www.guardian.co.uk/society/joepublic/2008/dec/10/child-protection-socialwork-baby-p (accessed 3 April 2009).

Finkelhor, D. and Browne, A. (1986) 'Initial and long-term effects: A conceptual framework', in D. Finkelhor (ed.), *A Sourcebook on Child Sexual Abuse*, pp. 180–98. Newbury Park, CA: Sage.

Fook, J. (1993) *Radical Casework: A Theory of Practice*. St Leonards, NSW: Allen and Unwin.

Fook, J. (1999) 'Critical reflectivity in education and practice', in B. Pease and J. Fook (eds), *Transforming Social Work Practice: Postmodern Critical Perspectives*, pp. 195–208. London: Routledge.

Fook, J. (2002) *Social Work: Critical Theory and Practice*. London: Sage.

Fook, J. and Pease, B. (1999) 'Emancipatory social work for a postmodern age', B. Pease and J. Fook (eds), *Transforming Social Work Practice: Postmodern Critical Perspectives*, pp. 224–9. London: Routledge.

Forrester, D., Kershaw, S., Moss, H. and Hughes, L. (2008) 'Communication skills in child protection: How do social workers talk to parents?', *Child and Family Social Work*, 13: 41–51.

Fox-Harding, L. (1991) 'The Children Act in context: Four perspectives in child care law and policy', *Journal of Social Welfare and Family Law*, 3: 179–93.

Furness, S. (2007) 'An enquiry into students' motivations to train as social workers in England', *Journal of Social Work*, 7(2): 239–53.

Gardner, R. (2008) *Developing an Effective Response to Neglect and Emotional Harm to Children*. Norwich: UEA and NSPCC.

Gibbons, J., Gallagher, B., Bell, C. and Gordon, D. (1995) *Development after Physical Abuse in Early Childhood*. London: HMSO.

Gould, N. (2003) 'The caring professions and information technology: In search of a theory', in E. Harlow and S. Webb (eds), *Information and Communication Technologies in the Welfare Services*. London: Jessica Kingsley Publishers.

Guardian (2008) *Baby P Timeline*. Available at: http://www.guardian.co.uk/
society/2008/dec/01/baby-p-timeline (accessed 3 April 2009).

Harris, J. (1998) 'Scientific management, bureau-professionalism, new managerialism: The labour process of state social work', *British Journal of
Social Work*, 28(6): 839–62.

Harris, J. (2003) *The Social Work Business*. London: Routledge.

Harris, N. (1987) 'Defensive social work', *British Journal of Social Work*,
17(1): 61–9.

Harris, R. (1997) 'Power', in *The Blackwell Companion to Social Work*, 1st
edn, pp. 28–33. Oxford: Blackwell.

Healy, K. (1998) 'Participation and child protection: The importance of
context', *British Journal of Social Work*, 28: 897–914.

Healy, K. (1999) 'Power and activist social work', in B. Pease and J. Fook
(eds), *Transforming Social Work Practice: Postmodern Critical Perspectives*, pp. 115–34. London: Routledge.

Healy, K. (2000) *Social Work Practices: Contemporary Perspectives on
Change*. London: Sage.

Healy, K. (2005) *Social Work Theories in Context: Creating Frameworks
for Practice*. Basingstoke: Palgrave Macmillan.

Healy, K. and Mulholland, J. (2007) *Writing Skills for Social Workers*.
London: Sage.

Hick, S., Fook, J. and Pozzuto, R. (eds) (2005) *Social Work: A Critical Turn*.
Ontario: Thompson Educational Publishing.

Hill, A. (2001) ' "No-one else could understand": Women's experiences of
a support group run by and for mothers of sexually abused children',
British Journal of Social Work, 31(3): 385–97.

Hill, A. (2003) 'Issues facing brothers of sexually abused children: Implications for professional practice', *Child and Family Social Work*, 8(4):
281–90.

HM Government (2006) *Working together to Safeguard Children: A Guide
to Inter-Agency Working to Safeguard and Promote the Welfare of Children*, London: TSO.

Holland, S. (2004) *Child and Family Assessment in Child Care Practice*.
London: Sage.

Holmes, J. (1993) *John Bowlby and Attachment Theory*. London:
Routledge.

Hooper, C. (1992) *Mothers Surviving Child Sexual Abuse*. London:
Routledge.

Horner, M. (2006) *What Is Social Work? Context and Perspectives*, 2nd
edn. Exeter: Learning Matters.

Horwath, J. and Morrison, T. (2000) 'Assessment of parental motivation to
change', in J. Horwath (ed.), *The Child's World: Assessing Children in
Need*, pp. 98–113. London: NSPCC.

Hughes, L. and Pengelly, P. (1997) *Staff Supervision in a Turbulent Environment*. London: Jessica Kingsley Publishers.

Ife, J. (1999) 'Postmodernism, critical theory and social work', in B. Pease and J. Fook (eds), *Transforming Social Work Practice: Postmodern Critical Perspectives*, pp. 211–23. London: Routledge.

Ivanoff, A., Blythe, B. and Tripodi, T. (1994) *Involuntary Clients in Social Work Practice*. New York: Aldine de Gruyter.

Jones, D. (2003) *Communicating with Vulnerable Children: A Guide for Practitioners*. London: Royal College of Psychiatrists.

Jordan, B. (1979) *Helping in Social Work*. London: Routledge and Kegan Paul.

Karvinen-Niinikoski, S. (2004) 'Social work supervision: Contributing to innovative knowledge production and open expertise', in N. Gould and M. Baldwin (eds), *Social Work, Critical Reflection and the Learning Organization*, pp. 23–39. Aldershot: Ashgate.

Kirkpatrick, I., Ackroyd, S. and Walker, R. (2005) *The New Managerialism and Public Service Professions: Change in Health, Social Services, and Housing*. Basingstoke: Palgrave Macmillan.

Knott, C. (2007) *Reflective Practice in Social Work*. Exeter: Learning Matters.

Koprowska, J. (2005) *Communication and Interpersonal Skills in Social Work*. Exeter: Learning Matters.

Laming, H. (2009) *The Protection of Children in England: A Progress Report*. London: The Stationery Office.

Langan, M. (2000) 'Social services: Managing the third way', in J. Clarke, S. Gewirtz and E. McLaughlin (eds), *New Managerialism, New Welfare*, pp. 152–68. London: Sage.

Latour, B. (1999) *Pandora's Hope: Essays on the Reality of Science Studies*. Cambridge, MA: Harvard University Press.

Mason, T. and Chandley, M. (1999) *Managing Violence and Aggression: A Manual for Nurses and Health Workers*. Edinburgh: Churchill Livingstone.

Mattinson, J. (1975) *The Reflection Process in Casework Supervision*. London: The Tavistock Institute of Human Relations.

McCracken, G. (1988) *The Long Interview*. Beverley Hills, CA: Sage.

McDonald, C. (2006) *Challenging Social Work: The Institutional Context of Practice*. Basingstoke: Palgrave Macmillan.

McLaren, H. (2007) 'Exploring the ethics of forewarning: Social workers, confidentiality and potential child abuse disclosures', *Ethics and Social Welfare*, 1(1): 22–40.

Menzies, I. (1988) 'The functioning of social systems as a defence against anxiety', in I. Menzies (ed.), *Selected Essays*. London: Free Association Books.

Miller, W. and Rollnick, S. (1991) *Motivational Interviewing: Preparing People to Change Addictive Behavior*. London: Guilford Press.

Ministry of Justice. (2002) 'Local authority social services act 1970: Schedule 1', *The UK Statute Law Database*. Available at: http://www.statutelaw.

gov.uk/content.aspx?LegType=All+Primary&PageNumber=1&NavFrom
=2&activeTextDocId=538583&parentActiveTextDocId=538583&linTo
ATDocumentId=477582&linkToATVersionNumber=17&showPr
osp=1&#81394 (accessed 19 July 2007).

Ministry of Justice and Judiciary of England and Wales (2008) *The Public Law Outline: Guide to Case Management in Public Law Proceedings.* Available at: http://www.judiciary.gov.uk/docs/public_law_outline.pdf, (accessed 27 May 2008).

Morrison, T. (2001) *Staff Supervision in Social Care: Making a Real Difference for Staff and Service Users.* Brighton: Pavilion Publishing.

Mullaly, B. (2007) *The New Structural Social Work*, 3rd edn. Ontario: Oxford University Press.

Munro, E. (1998) 'Improving social worker's knowledge base in child protection work', *British Journal of Social Work*, 28: 89–105.

Murdin, L. (2000) *How Much Is Enough? Endings in Psychotherapy and Counselling.* London: Routledge.

National Task Force on Violence against Social Care Staff (2000) *Report and National Action Plan.* Available at: http://www.dh.gov.uk/en/Publicationsandstatistics/Publications/PublicationsPolicyandGuidance/DH_4010625 (accessed 25 March 2008).

Obholzer, A. and Roberts, V. (eds) (1994) *The Unconscious at Work: Individual and Organisational Stress in the Human Services.* Hove: Branner-Routledge.

Parker, S., Fook, J. and Pease, B. (1999) 'Empowerment: The modernist social work concept par excellence', in B. Pease and J. Fook (eds), *Transforming Social Work Practice: Postmodern Critical Perspectives*, pp. 150–7. London: Routledge.

Parrott, L. (2006) *Values and Ethics in Social Work Practice.* Exeter: Learning Matters.

Parton, N. (1998) 'Risk, advanced liberalism and child welfare: The need to rediscover uncertainty and ambiguity', *British Journal of Social Work*, 28(1): 5–27.

Payne, M. (2006) *What Is Professional Social Work?* 2nd edn. Bristol: Policy Press.

Pease, B. and Fook, J. (eds) (1999) *Transforming Social Work Practice: Postmodern Critical Perspectives.* London: Routledge.

Penna, S. (2005) 'The Children Act 2004: Child protection and social surveillance', *Journal of Social Welfare and Family Law*, 27(2): 143–57.

Pincus, A. and Minahan, A. (1973) *Social Work Practice: Model and Method.* Itasca, IL: F. E. Peacock.

Pinker, R. (1990) *Social Work in an Enterprise Society.* London: Routledge.

Prochaska, J. and DiClemente, C. (1982) 'Trans-theoretical therapy: Toward a more integrative model of change', *Psychotherapy, Theory, Research and Practice*, 19(3): 276–88.

Reamer, F. (2005) 'Documentation in social work: Evolving ethical and risk management standards', *Social Work*, 50(4): 325–34.

Reder, P., Duncan, S. and Gray, M. (1993) *Beyond Blame: Child Abuse Tragedies Revisited*. London: Routledge.

Rogers, A. and Pilgrim, D. (2001) *Mental Health Policy in Britain*, 2nd edn. Basingstoke: Palgrave Macmillan.

Rogers, C. (1961) *On Becoming a Person*. Boston, MA: Houghton Mifflin.

Rooney, R. (1992) *Strategies for Work with Involuntary Clients*. New York: Columbia University Press.

Ruch, G. (2007) 'Reflective practice in contemporary child-care social work: The role of containment', *British Journal of Social Work*, 37: 659–80.

Salter, A. (1988) *Treating Child Sex Offenders and Victims: A Practical Guide*. Newbury Park, CA: Sage.

Schön, D. (1995) *The Reflective Practitioner: How Professionals Think in Action*. Aldershot: Arena.

Seden, J. (2001) *Studies Informing the Framework for the Assessment of Children in Need and Their Families*. London: The Stationery Office.

Seymour, C. and Seymour, R. (2007) *Courtroom Skills for Social Workers*. Exeter: Learning Matters.

Shaw, I. (1996) *Evaluating in Practice*. Aldershot: Arena.

Shaw, I. (1999) *Qualitative Evaluation*. London: Sage.

Smith, G. (1995) 'Assessing protectiveness in cases of child sexual abuse', in L. Reder and C. Lucey (eds), *Assessment of Parenting*, pp. 87–101. London: Routledge.

Smith, R. (2007) *Youth Justice: Ideas, Policy, Practice*. Cullompton: Willan.

Stephenson, O. (1989) *Child Abuse: Professional Practice and Public Policy*. Hemel Hempstead: Harvester Wheatsheaf.

Symington, J. and Symington, N. (1996) *The Clinical Thinking of Wilfred Bion*. London: Routledge.

Tasker, F. and Bigner, J. (2007) *Gay and Lesbian Parenting: New Directions*. New York: Haworth Press.

Thompson, N. (2005) *Understanding Social Work: Preparing for Practice*, 2nd edn. Basingstoke: Palgrave Macmillan.

Thompson, N. (2006) *Anti-Discriminatory Practice*, 4th edn. Basingstoke: Palgrave Macmillan.

Thorburn, J., Lewis, A. and Shemmings, D. (1995) *Paternalism or Partnership? Family Involvement in the Child Protection Process*. London: HMSO.

Trevillion, S. (1992) *Caring in the Community: A Networking Approach to Community Partnership*. Harlow: Longman.

Trevithick, P. (2005) *Social Work Skills: A Practice Handbook*, 2nd edn. Maidenhead: Open University Press.

Trevithick, P., Richards, S., Ruch, G. and Moss, M. (2004) *Teaching and Learning Communication Skills in Social Work Education: Knowledge Review 6*. London: Social Care Institute for Excellence.

Trotter, C. (2006) *Working with Involuntary Clients: A Guide to Practice*, 2nd edn. London: Sage.

Tsui, M. (2005) *Social Work Supervision: Contexts and Concepts*. Thousand Oaks, CA: Sage.

Turnell, A., Lohrbach, S. and Curran, S. (2008) 'Working with involuntary clients in child protection: Lessons from successful practice', in M. Calder (ed.), *The Carrot or the Stick? Towards Effective Practice with Involuntary Clients in Safeguarding Children Work*, pp. 104–15. Lyme Regis: Russell House Publishing.

Walker, S. and Beckett, C. (2003) *Social Work Assessment and Intervention*. Lyme Regis: Russell House Publishing.

Wilson, A. and Beresford, P. (2000) ' "Anti-oppressive practice": Emancipation or appropriation?', *British Journal of Social Work*, 30: 553–753.

Wilson, K., Kendrick, P. and Ryan, V. (1992) *Play Therapy; A Non-Directive Approach for Children and Adolescents*. London: Ballière Tindall.

Wilson, K., Ruch, G., Lymbery, M. and Cooper, A. (2008) *Social Work: An Introduction to Contemporary Practice*. Harlow: Pearson.

Yatchmenoff, D. (2008) 'A closer look at client engagement: Understanding and assessing engagement from the perspectives of workers and clients in non-voluntary child protective services', in M. Calder (ed.), *The Carrot or the Stick? Towards Effective Practice with Involuntary Clients in Safeguarding Children Work*, pp. 59–77. Lyme Regis: Russell House Publishing.

Youth Justice Board. (2006) *Asset – Young Offender Assessment Profile*. Available at: http://www.yjb.gov.uk/en-gb/practitioners/Assessment/Asset.htm (accessed 12 August 2008).

Index